RALPH NADER

Recent Titles in Greenwood Biographies

RALPH NADER

A Biography

Patricia Cronin Marcello

GREENWOOD BIOGRAPHIES

GREENWOOD PRESS
WESTPORT, CONNECTICUT · LONDON

Library of Congress Cataloging-in-Publication Data

Marcello, Patricia Cronin.
    Ralph Nader : a biography / Patricia Cronin Marcello.
        p. cm. — (Greenwood biographies)
    Includes bibliographical references.
    ISBN 0–313–33004–2 (hardcover : alk. paper)
    1. Nader, Ralph. 2. Consumer affairs directors—United States—Biography.
3. Lobbyists—United States—Biography. 4. Presidential candidates—United States—
Biography. 5. Consumer protection—United States. I. Title. II. Series.
HC110.C63M367 2004
    343.7307'1'092—dc22   2004012493

British Library Cataloguing in Publication Data is available.

Library of Congress Catalog Card Number: 2004012493

ISBN: 0–313–33004–2
ISSN: 1540–4900

First published in 2004

Greenwood Press, 88 Post Road West, Westport, CT 06881
An imprint of Greenwood Publishing Group, Inc.
www.greenwood.com

Printed in the United States of America

The paper used in this book complies with the
Permanent Paper Standard issued by the National
Information Standards Organization (Z39.48–1984).

10   9   8   7   6   5   4   3   2   1

To Patrick, for without him, there would be no books,
To Shannon, who never ceases to amaze and delight me, and
To Pearl, who stuck so close to me, as I wrote this book. May she rest.

CONTENTS

Photo essay follows page 80.

SERIES FOREWORD

In response to high school and public library needs, Greenwood developed this distinguished series of full-length biographies specifically for student use. Prepared by field experts and professionals, these engaging biographies are tailored for high school students who need challenging yet accessible biographies. Ideal for secondary school assignments, the length, format and subject areas are designed to meet educators' requirements and students' interests.

Greenwood offers an extensive selection of biographies spanning all curriculum related subject areas including social studies, the sciences, literature and the arts, history and politics, as well as popular culture, covering public figures and famous personalities from all time periods and backgrounds, both historic and contemporary, who have made an impact on American and/or world culture. Greenwood biographies were chosen based on comprehensive feedback from librarians and educators. Consideration was given to both curriculum relevance and inherent interest. The result is an intriguing mix of the well known and the unexpected, the saints and sinners from long-ago history and contemporary pop culture. Readers will find a wide array of subject choices from fascinating crime figures like Al Capone to inspiring pioneers like Margaret Mead, from the greatest minds of our time like Stephen Hawking to the most amazing success stories of our day like J. K. Rowling.

While the emphasis is on fact, not glorification, the books are meant to be fun to read. Each volume provides in-depth information about the subject's life from birth through childhood, the teen years, and adulthood. A thorough account relates family background and education, traces personal and professional influences, and explores struggles, accomplishments, and contributions. A timeline highlights the most significant life events against a historical perspective. Bibliographies supplement the reference value of each volume.

INTRODUCTION

Ralph Nader is not an enigma. He is the product of immigrant parents, who knew the value of life in America. He was taught by both parents to love the land in which we live and to work toward making it a better place for all. Much as a monk dedicates his life to spirituality, Ralph Nader has dedicated his life to good citizenship and showing others how to put democracy into action.

It all began nearly four decades ago, when Nader saw the need for manufacturers to work toward more than pure profit. He forced them to be responsible to those who bought products, through coercion from the federal legislature. At first, it seemed that this was the most effective solution.

Yet, over time, Nader realized that even Congress had become beholden to the very companies being censured. He recognized the need for grassroots support for the issues he was bound by duty of citizenship to attack. The Center for the Study of Responsive Law, Public Citizen, Essential Information, the Center for Auto Safety, Citizen Works, and Trial Lawyers for Public Justice are only a few of the organizations that Nader has in part or wholly begun. He mobilized people to demand safer cars, cheaper home heating oil, more wholesome meat and poultry, and in California, an instant 20 percent reduction in auto and home insurance rates.

Nader is not a saint to all, however. To some, he is the leader in the current trend to litigate cases beyond common sense. Many in Congress see him as a spoiler of elections and a nuisance. He's even been hit in the face with a pie. Yet, he carries on with the fervor of Thomas Paine, the rage of Upton Sinclair, and the energy of an atom, affecting all he touches. Nader is the conscience and the will of tacitly approving American people. He will not be ignored.

Through his prolific writing, since his days at Princeton and Harvard Law, he has tackled issues with the help of his infamous Nader's Raiders. The books that he endorsed include volumes on clean air and water, Congressional and federal agency reviews, and his famous *Unsafe at Any Speed*, which brought Nader to the public's attention. In 2004, he is once again in the public's face, asking for the presidency of the United States.

Like him or hate him, one thing is certain. Ralph Nader is well intentioned. He believes fully in every cause he battles and will battle where others, beholden to the endorsements of big business, fear to tread. He is in it for America, and his vigor in that pursuit will never wane.

In forming this work, research was gathered from various primary sources, such as Harold A. Katz, Esq., the author of an article that helped ignite Nader's interest in auto safety. Professor Laura Nader grew up with Ralph and wrote to me of their family bonds and responsibilities as citizens. Lallie Lloyd was a Maiden Muckraker, whose road to adult independence began with a study initiated by Nader, and Deck Deckert, formerly of the *Miami Herald* and author of Nader-related articles and other books, supports Nader with admirable courage of conviction. To them, I offer my thanks. I would also like to thank Ralph Nader for giving me his most valuable time and for discussing important issues not seen in other publications. His words are the lifeblood of this book.

My research also included government documents and secondary sources, such as books by Nader and others, magazine and newspaper articles, and newsletters. I also employed reliable sites on the World Wide Web; URLs are listed in endnotes and the bibliography. All these sources meshed to enable me to perform the enormous task of rendering a portrait of Nader's complicated life story in only one book.

TIMELINE: EVENTS IN THE LIFE OF RALPH NADER

27 February 1934	Ralph Nader is born in Winsted, Connecticut
1937	Travels to Lebanon with mother and siblings
September 1939	Enters Mary P. Hinsdale Elementary School
October 1941	Begins lifelong interest in baseball with World Series
September 1944	Enters Central School (now Pearson Middle School)
September 1947	Begins high school at the Gilbert School in Winsted
1949	Carries newspapers for the *Winsted Evening Citizen*
June 1951	Graduates from Gilbert School with honors
September 1951	Enters Princeton University
June 1955	Graduates magna cum laude from Princeton
Summer 1955	Works at Yosemite National Park
19 August 1955	Mad River floods, damaging family restaurant business in Winsted
September 1955	Enters Harvard Law School
27 October 1955	Joins staff of *Harvard Law School Record*; gets first byline
1955	Harold A. Katz writes article on auto safety for the *Harvard Law Review*, helping to ignite Nader's interest in the subject
June 1958	Graduates from Harvard Law School then joins the United States Army Reserve for six months

April 1959	Travels to Cuba where he attends press conference of Fidel Castro
11 April 1959	"The Safe Car You Can't Buy" published in *The Nation*
Summer 1961	Travels to Scandinavia to learn more about ombudsman system
May–September 1963	Visits Latin America
1964	Senator Daniel P. Moynihan invites Ralph to join his planning staff, regarding the issue of auto safety in Washington, D.C.
January 1965	Begins to suspect General Motors of harassment
30 November 1965	*Unsafe at Any Speed, the Designed-In Dangers of the American Automobile,* Nader's first book, published
10 February 1966	Testifies before the Subcommittee on Executive Reorganization of the Committee on Government Operations regarding auto safety
13 February 1966	Report of Nader being followed appears in *Washington Post*
22 March 1966	James M. Roche, Chairman and CEO of General Motors, apologizes to Nader at congressional hearing
14 November 1966	Nader files suit against General Motors for harassment
Summer 1967	"We Are Still in the Jungle" and "Watch That Hamburger" regarding unwholesome meat packaging appear in *The New Republic*
15 December 1967	Wholesome Meat Act signed into law by President Lyndon B. Johnson
22 January 1968	Nader on cover of *Newsweek*
June 1968	Assembles group of young lawyers to investigate consumer issues, later to be dubbed "Nader's Raiders"
6 January 1969	Raiders' report on the Federal Trade Commission is published
May 1969	Begins involvement with United Mine Workers' election to defeat W. A. "Tony" Boyle
Summer 1969	Founds Center for Study of Responsive Law Study on Interstate Commerce Commission published

	Vanishing Air published, insulting Senator Edmund Muskie
20 November 1969	Speaks at Miss Porter's School, Farmington, Connecticut
1970	Loses faith in Congress to pass adequate legislation and turns efforts to grass roots organizing
7 February 1970	Endorses Campaign GM
June 1970	Maiden Muckrakers begin investigation of nursing homes in Washington, D.C.
August 1970	Establishes first Public Interest Research Group (PIRG)
13 August 1970	Settles lawsuit against GM for invasion of privacy, receives $425,000
30 January 1971	Holds Whistle-blowing Conference at Mayflower Hotel
18 April 1971	Receives Max Berg Award
31 October 1971	Letter in *New York Times*, asking for contributions to initiate Public Citizen
1 November 1971	The Congress Project announcement
1 January 1972	*The Closed Enterprise System*, regarding antitrust enforcement is published
June 1972	The Congress Project begins
August 1972	Nader declines to be George McGovern's running partner in presidential election
October 1972	Congress Project findings released
1973	Establishes Congress Watch
16–18 November 1974	Critical Mass conference held at Statler Hilton, Washington, D.C.
1975	Anti-Nader sentiments begin to rise. *Hit and Run: The Rise—and Fall?—of Ralph Nader* by Ralph de Toledano published
7–8 August 1976	Visits Jimmy Carter in Plains, Georgia
15 January 1977	Hosts *Saturday Night Live*
June 1977	Involved in massive push for Consumer Protection Agency (CPA)
8 February 1978	CPA bill defeated in House; Nader blames Carter
March 1978	FANS article published in *Playboy*
1979	First Residential Utility Consumer Action Group (RUCAG) established in Wisconsin

November 1980	Ronald Reagan elected as President
January 1981	Reagan begins deregulation, unraveling much of what Nader had accomplished
1982	Nader founds Essential Information and helps to found Trial Lawyers for Public Justice
1983	Forms Buyers Up and first national PIRG organization
11 June 1985	Speaks at Harvard Law School
1986	Develops Bell's palsy
August 1986	Shafeek Nader dies; Ralph goes into seclusion for three months
1987	Interviewed by *Rolling Stone*
1988	Fights for Proposition 103 in California
1989	Founds Princeton Project 55 and fights for ownership of Taxpayer Assets, including airwaves
1991	The debate over NAFTA and GATT begin
1992	Nader runs for the presidential election as a non-candidate
October 1995	Nader considers entering the presidential primary in California
19 August 1995	The Green Party elects Nader for their candidate; Nader chooses Winona LaDuke for his running mate
November 1995	Receives one percent of the popular vote in the presidential election
December 1999	Begins considering another run for the presidency
21 February 2000	Nader announces his candidacy
5 November 2000	Gains 2.74 percent of popular vote in presidential election
2001	Involved in anti-Microsoft campaigning
2002	Enron collapse; Nader weighs in on corporate crime and punishment
mid-August 2003	Nader considering another run for the Presidency
23 February 2004	Nader proclaims himself an Independent candidate in the presidential race
21 June 2004	Selects Peter Miguel Camejo as vice presidential running mate

Chapter 1

A FOUNDATION FOR SOCIAL CONSCIENCE

Most boys dream of becoming doctors, firemen, or astronauts, but Ralph Nader only dreamed of becoming a lawyer. Sitting in courtrooms with his father from the time he was a small boy, Nader saw the legal system in action and firmly decided on his career before he was in middle school. Civics was more than a day trip for the Nader family; it was a way of life.

Nathra, Nader's father, was born in Lebanon in 1892. Nathra's father had died when Nathra was very young, and as a child, Nathra helped to support his family, in part, by playing marbles for money. He grew into a tall, lean young man with restless energy and a sizzling personality.

Nathra came to the United States in 1912 at age 19 with only about $20 (U.S.) to support himself. Nathra knew little English and had only a sixth-grade education, but he was industrious and worked different jobs in different parts of the country to earn his living. In Detroit, he worked at the Maxwell Auto Works. In Massachusetts, he worked in a machine shop, and in New Jersey, he was employed by a shoe factory.

Nathra saved his money, and in 1924, was ready to return to Lebanon to marry the woman he had been promised—Rose Bouzaine of Zahle, a diminutive woman with light skin and very dark eyes. One of eight daughters, Rose was raised in a sod-roof house with white walls and nomadic rugs covering tile floors. Her family farmed and tended sheep, and she fondly remembers everyone gathered in the kitchen, which was always bustling with food preparation and laughter.

Rose's education was intended to lead her into teaching. Of the eight daughters in her family, six of them became teachers, including Rose, and her first teaching assignment took her away from home. The town was hours away from Zahle, but the adventurous Rose left her family to begin her adult life.

At the time Rose left home, the influenza pandemic, in which between 20 and 40 million people died worldwide, was in full force, and it had gripped the town where Rose taught. In fact, her whole class had become infected. The doctor warned Rose not to visit her students for fear that she would contract the virus herself. However, Rose's compassion would not allow her to ignore the children, and she visited them anyway. She wrote, "I found them in their homes lying on their mattresses stretched out on the floor, and I brought them water and talked to them."[1] She credits her ability to maintain good health despite the highly contagious influenza with eating plenty of garlic.

A RADICAL CHANGE

When her teaching contract was up in 1925, Rose entered her marriage with Nathra Nader, which had been arranged years before. Rose joined a new husband, and she detached from her roots. She was destined to leave her country for a new home in America. No longer would she teach the children of strangers. She would prepare to raise a family of her own.

For the first year of their marriage, the couple lived in Danbury, Connecticut, but was not pleased with the surroundings. They wanted a more pastoral setting in which to raise their children, so they moved to Winsted, about 43 miles due northeast of Danbury, at the confluence of the Still and Mad Rivers.

Founded in 1871, Winsted is known as the Laurel City and for the Gilbert Clock factory, named for local clockmaker William L. Gilbert. At the time the Naders moved to Winsted, the factory was Winsted's largest employer. Winsted is also known for the Winchester's Soldiers' Monument, dedicated on September 11, 1890, as a testimony to the soldiers from the surrounding area who fought and died in the Civil War.

The Naders soon bought a white house on Hillside Avenue, which looked out on the hill where the monument sits on Crown Avenue. Built in 1917, the house had two stories and ten rooms. Nathra had always wanted his own business, so he opened a confectionary called the Highland Sweet Shop on the town's Main Street, which soon became a restaurant known as the Highland Arms.

The eatery became Nathra's pulpit. Whenever someone brought up an issue, or even when no one did, Nathra would expound on his views to anyone who might listen. Once, he asked a doctor how he billed his clients; the doctor replied that he asked what the patient could afford. Nathra said, "I like that! For you, the martini is five dollars. For a poor man, it is ten cents."[2]

The Naders' first three children—Shafeek, born in 1926; Claire, born 1929; and Laura, born in 1932—all came into the world at the house on Hillside Avenue. When her fourth child was to be born, Rose was determined to deliver in a hospital. At least in a maternity ward, she would be able to rest and recuperate. However, nature would not let Rose have her way. On February 27, 1934, when she went into labor, a raging blizzard was in progress, and because she could not get to a hospital, the last Nader child, Ralph, was also born at home.

ON BEING A NADER

The Naders were nurturing parents. Rose always made sure that the family ate foods that were good for the body. Sodas were out, and even sugar was not part of the children's regular diet. In fact, whenever there was a birthday, Rose would frost and decorate the cake, but as soon as the candles were blown out, she would remove the icing before serving it to guests and family. She wrote, "They don't have to like what they eat, they just have to eat it. Parents should eat the same food; no double standard."[3]

When Nader was about three years old, his father fulfilled a promise he had made to Rose's family that during the first 15 years of marriage, he would allow her to return to Lebanon for a visit. So, Rose and her children sailed to Lebanon while Nathra stayed behind to run the restaurant.

The children were excited to meet their Lebanese family; both Arabic and English were spoken at home and the children were fluent in both languages, so communicating would be no problem. So that the Nader children would not fall behind in school, their aunts, who were teachers, tutored them. During their stay, they visited the town of Arsoun, where their father was raised, and their father's family house there. They were surprised to find that it faced a mountain, just as the Winsted home faced a steep hill.

When they returned home, the school board was reluctant to allow Nader to enter first grade because he spoke a mixture of Arabic and English. They worried that he would not be able to keep up with his peer group, but Rose strongly urged them to reconsider. She knew Nader was quite ready to enter school, and at her urging, the school board relented. Nader entered the first grade at Mary P. Hinsdale Elementary School in

September 1939, where he would spend his first five years of formal education.

Nader proved to be an excellent student, and though instructors were only teaching addition and subtraction, Nader asked his teacher for a book to learn multiplication and division. His mother had already primed him on the simpler operations at home.

While the children were still in grade school, the Naders, especially Nathra, would institute discussions of current events, politics, and civic consciousness. Of his zeal, Laura Nader said,

> My father's most passionate issue was justice—after all, Lebanon was colonized by the Ottomans, by the French; such colonization included the rest of the Arab world and included other European powers like the British. [My father] had made the USA his new home and country and was as passionate about justice through law here as elsewhere. I was not intimidated by my father—he helped his children to learn how to think critically. He could see in front of him how big business was destroying small businesses, family businesses. So could we.[4]

All the children were expected to weigh in with rational opinions. Nathra would analyze the response and further question each of the children until they were involved in a lively discussion, and the conversation could range from religion to the state of the Union. None of the children were permitted to become upset about heated discussions. Nader's sister Claire recalled, "We were never allowed to run under fire.... You had to stand your ground and talk it out."[5]

Rose taught more through parables than discussion and wanted the children to be self-reliant and individualistic. Nader was forced to endure short pants until he was eight years old and suffered teasing at the hands of the other boys in his class. When he complained to his mother about the situation and argued that the other boys wore long pants, she said, "So, you're different, other children have their mothers and you have yours."[6] She then asked him if he was a leader or a follower. This separation from the group would continue to be a pattern in Nader's life.

Nathra and Rose taught thrift to their children as well. Each week, the children were given a dime—not an allowance, but an amount intended for saving. Each week, they were expected to march down to the local bank and deposit the money into their savings accounts. Whenever the children wanted something, they had to ask their parents for it.

MATURING AND GROWING

For sixth through eighth grades, Nader moved on to Central School, now Pearson Middle School. Already a voracious reader by this time, his older brother Shafeek provided Nader with a reading list, which included such classics as *Moby Dick*. Nader also enjoyed Westerns by Zane Grey, the autobiography of Helen Keller, and even Chinese history. Most fascinating for him, however, were the works of Upton Sinclair, who wrote *The Jungle*, an exposé of abuses in the meat packing industry; Ida Tarbell, author of *The History of the Standard Oil Company*, a work uncovering how John D. Rockefeller used illegal means to create a monopoly in the early oil industry; Lincoln Steffens, who wrote *The Struggle for Self-Government*, an investigation of state politics; and George Seldes, author of *Tell the Truth and Run* and *Never Tire of Protesting*. These investigative journalists were known as muckrakers because their work incited further scrutiny of the issues they had tackled. They had even motivated Congress to pass legislation because of their diligent efforts to uncover the truth. The writings of the muckrakers inspired Nader, and he began to contemplate the distribution of power in America.

About this time, Shafeek also taught Nader to love baseball, and Nader became an avid fan with the World Series of 1941. In Winsted, because Connecticut lacked its own team, residents were either fans of the Red Sox or the Yankees. Nader became a devoted Yankee fan. At age seven, he perceived the Yankees to be the underdogs. He had not realized that by that time the team, which was started in 1903, was a powerhouse, having already won several world championships. When he learned this fact, he was already a well-ensconced Yankee fan. He remarked, "I followed every game, knew all the stats."[7]

Nader also liked to play baseball and played many pick-up games with kids in his neighborhood. Often included in this group was David Halberstam, Pulitzer Prize–winning journalist and author of such books as *The Fifties* and *The Best and the Brightest*, a look at how the United States got into the war in Vietnam. Halberstam also went to school with Nader from the fourth through the eighth grades.

Halberstam remembers a certain amount of animosity between the Jews and Arabs in Winsted at the time the boys were growing up. He said, "It was a different generation. The Jews felt the Arabs were anti-Semitic, not feeling that they, the Jews, might be anti-Arab."[8] Yet, these feelings never bothered the children, who played together as equals. In Halberstam's mind, there was no question that Nader had no bias against Jews, though he was of Arabic origin. For the kids, race or descendency was not an issue.

At age 13, Nader entered the Gilbert School for 9th to 12th grades. Founded by clockmaker William L. Gilbert, the school's purpose was to endow education "for the improvement of mankind by affording such assistance and means of educating the young as will help them to become good citizens."[9] At the time Nader was a student at the high school, it was a Victorian building of yellow brick; however, a new Gilbert School was erected in 1959.

While in high school, Nader was a virtual ghost. He kept to himself, and though he did join the drama club, he worked behind the scenes alone. He did have some friends, but as studious types, they were considered the eggheads. Although Nader spoke his mind in the classroom, he was never disrespectful to teachers. Because of his nightly discussions around the family dinner table, Nader could usually enhance any classroom discussion.

In his first year of high school, Nader did something few people would do, let alone kids his age. He brought home a stack of *Congressional Records* that his principal gave to him because no one else read them. Nader poured over them voraciously, learning much about how Congress works.

Nader never participated in dances or parties and showed no interest in dating. He played chess often. When he graduated in 1951, his yearbook photo caption read, "quiet—smart—can be found either at home or at the restaurant—woman-hater."[10] The yearbook staff was being extreme; Nader just had no interest in the opposite sex. Unlike other boys his age, Nader was serious and, through his parents' teaching, only concerned with learning to be the best citizen he could be. The only way to achieve that was by dedicating himself to hard work at school. "Success was not a word I heard at home," said Laura Nader. "Purpose was central, as was the need to do a good job at whatever we did and to contribute to the larger society."[11]

Nader graduated with honors from the Gilbert School in 1951, and though he had considered Harvard, Swarthmore, and Haverford colleges, he chose Princeton for his undergraduate studies because of the university's strong oriental languages department. He majored in Far East politics and languages and took courses in Chinese and Russian.

Though Nader would have qualified for an academic scholarship, Nathra would not hear of his applying. Nathra felt that scholarships should be for young people whose parents could not afford to pay tuition, and as the restaurant was doing well, Nathra footed the bill for all of his children's college educations. Only Shafeek returned to work in the family restaurant in Winsted, where he also became a devoted activist to his hometown.

AMONG THE IVY-COVERED WALLS OF PRINCETON

Although Nader found the Ivy League atmosphere at Princeton welcoming, he also found it puzzling. All the facilities for a top-notch experience of the mind were available, but the all-male population at that time had decided that studying was not "cool." Nader's continued eggheadedness automatically set him apart from the Princeton crowd. Yet, he was making a statement by studying hard and being the best student he could be.

Actually, Nader liked the fact that he was different. Rather than don the Princeton chic of the Silent Generation[12] by wearing khaki pants, a white Oxford cloth, button-down shirt, an expensive blazer, and scuffed white suede oxford shoes, Nader was happy in the peacoat his brother Shafeek, who served in the Navy during World War II, had given him. One day, Nader even protested the Princeton "uniform" by appearing in class in a bathrobe.

As a freshman, his first room was on the ground floor and cost 35 dollars a month. It was the cheapest room on campus. He liked it because he could crawl out the window, rather than use the door, and continue on to his class. He considered it a unique way to begin his day.

His start at Princeton did not exactly go off as planned, however. Nader missed his first class because he had stayed up reading until four o'clock in the morning. But this pattern did not continue, and he worked extremely hard over the next four years. One of his favorite haunts was the library, with hundreds of books in open stacks. Nader was a voracious reader and filled most idle hours with books.

Nader hitchhiked everywhere, even to Winsted. Rather than take the bus, he spent several hours with his thumb out, waiting for rides. The times were much different then, and hitchhiking was safer and an inexpensive way of getting around. Nader saw many interesting things on the road, and sometimes, tragedy. Once, he witnessed an accident where an infant had nearly been decapitated by a glove compartment door that had sprung open on impact. The incident affected his life greatly, although he had no idea how strong his outrage over carnage on the highway would become for several more years.

Among Nader's friends at Princeton were Theodore (Ted) Jacobs, another studious soul, and Bill Shafer, another solid baseball fan. In their sophomore year, they all participated in the annual rite of "the bicker," rather like fraternity rushes, where fraternities evaluate underclassmen for inclusion in their group. Fraternities were banned at Princeton in 1855. Instead, the prestigious university has its eating clubs, with names such as the Cap and Gown, the Campus, and the Charter clubs. When Nader was at Princeton, a student had to be invited to be considered for membership in most eating clubs. Only two clubs—the Prospect and the Court—required no invitation. Nader joined the Prospect Club, the only club on campus where the students took turns sharing server duties, whereas other clubs had professional wait staffs.

In Nader's sophomore year, he entered the Woodrow Wilson School of Public and International Affairs, affectionately known as Woody Wood by the students. Nader had received the highest grades in his freshman year and his application to study at Woody Wood was accepted. His course load was also heavy with far eastern studies, economics, and Middle Eastern studies. For these studies, he traveled again to Lebanon for his paper "Some of the Problems in the Economic Development of Lebanon."

ACTIVISM AND EXPLORATION

When Nader was a junior, he was walking to class one day when he noticed a trail of dead birds lining his route and realized that the same thing had happened each of the two previous springs at Princeton, around the same time that DDT was sprayed to stifle the mosquito population. He speculated that if the DDT killed birds, it must also be harmful to the students.

Nader wrote several letters to the student newspaper, the *Daily Princetonian*, regarding this conclusion, but his letters went unnoticed. Fed up with the blatant disregard of the problem, he took a dead bird to the newspaper offices and presented it to the editor. In a subsequent letter to the *Daily Princetonian*, Nader wrote that the editor's reaction was apathetic, and described it as: "If it was harmful, *they* wouldn't do it." And he then wrote that the editor's attitude was "A perfect case of the insults men will tolerate if they're conditioned to trust the system."[13]

Nader graduated magna cum laude, and his professors urged him to continue his studies and obtain his Ph.D. Nader had not changed his mind about careers, however—he still wanted to become a lawyer. He had been accepted at Harvard Law School and would not be persuaded to veer off the course.

Wanting to have an adventure before tackling more hard studies, Nader took a trip out West at the suggestion of his sister Laura. He shared a ride with a medical student who had been hired to drive the car to Los Angeles. Along the way, the two stopped at the Hopi and Navajo reservations in Arizona, which fascinated Nader. Yet, when they reached Los Angeles, Nader needed to make a living, so he traveled north and took a job as a day laborer in an apricot grove, where he met many fascinating people. He loved the atmosphere in the barracks where he and the other workers slept.

Eventually, Nader moved on to San Francisco, but could find no work. He heard that there was work in Yosemite National Park, about 142 miles due east of San Francisco. When he arrived, Nader had very little money. He found work at a grocery store, but had to live in a tent outside a ranger's station before he could eventually move to a dormitory. When he was not working, he was hiking the trails and soaking up the atmosphere and stories from folks he met along the way.

TIMES OF TRAGEDY AND DISAPPOINTMENT

All was going well until Nader saw a story in the local newspaper. On August 19, 1955, the Mad River had overflowed its banks back in Winsted, creating a terrible flood, which washed out most of Winsted's main street and killed three people. In the wake of two simultaneous hurricanes—Connie and Diane—more than a foot of rainwater had fallen over parts of New England in just a few hours. Although Nader tried to phone home, the lines were down, so he headed off for Connecticut immediately.

Not until he reached Chicago was he able to speak with his family to find that the Highland Arms had suffered serious damage. Had it been on the other side of Main Street, however, it would have been destroyed. A disaster loan helped rebuild the Naders' business, and the restaurant stayed open for many more years.

Still, the disaster changed things for Nader. For the first time, he would need to apply for a scholarship to meet tuition payments for law school. It may have been the second omen of a rocky start at Harvard. The first incident had been Nader's poor performance on the entrance exam. Although he was admitted anyway, because of his stellar grades at Princeton, Nader insisted on taking the test again, just to prove to himself that he could do better and he did. The last and most damning element of Nader's rocky start was his own first impression of the school.

Nader found Harvard cold, urban, and not at all like Princeton. He said, "Everything was towers, vertical, cramped. It was very uncomfortable."[14] He was also appalled by the overall mental narrowness and moral complacency at the school. This impression and his physical discomfort would color all three years of his tenure at Harvard. Where he had been the model student at Princeton, he became the supreme slacker at Harvard and graduated in the lower half of his class.

Nader cut classes as a regular practice and would often disappear for days at a time, much to the despair of his teachers. And if he did not like a particular instructor, he attended the same class taught by another professor. He did his studying late into the night, slept late into the morning, and became increasingly antisocial.

Because of his father's financial setback, Nader also had to take on a variety of part-time jobs. He was a fast typist, so he typed papers for other students. He was the afternoon manager of a bowling alley in Harvard Square, and he imported inlaid metal boxes from Lebanon and handmade shawls from Mexico and sold them to other students and the public. Nader also saved money by buying only a partial food ticket and getting his roommate, Ed Levin, to smuggle fruit back to the dorm for him.

Soon after his arrival in Cambridge, Nader sold the only automobile he ever owned, a 1949 Studebaker, and resumed his habit of walking or hitchhiking to get around the city. Near the end of his first year at Harvard, Nader also dropped out of the dorms and lived off campus; fellow students saw him as becoming increasingly secretive. Yet, Nader believes that personal privacy is intertwined with our right of free speech and that when others know too much about a person, they will begin to question that person's motives or to have biases against what the person says because they know something about his or her private life. Already in law school, he seemed to have started his preparation for his lifelong mission and was adamant about people not knowing much about him.

During his time at Harvard, Nader also took frequent trips and came back to campus only in time for an exam. Once, because he heard that his sister Laura was suffering from malaria, he flew to Mexico, yet he never made it. He got to Oaxaca and came down with a severe case of dysentery that accompanied a relapse into malaria, which he had first caught while visiting Naples, Italy, years earlier. Laura became sufficiently well to travel and went to her brother's side to minister to him, rather than the other way around. Laura Nader said, "To support each other, to take care of each other is essential to what it means to be a sibling and what family means. My parents did not have an *individuated* model, which to my mind cancels out what family means. This does not mean that each child did not have their own dreams, just that such dreams are more meaningful if part of a family."[15] Such close ties and an astute awareness of the world provided

Nader with the confidence he needed to share his views with anyone who could read or listen.

THE POWER OF WRITING

Nader is a prolific writer to this day, and the groundwork for this practice was laid in his years at Harvard. As one of his early acts, he joined the staff of the *Harvard Law School Record* on October 27, 1955, and got his first byline on an article criticizing capital punishment. His next piece was a long, 6,000-word article about the plight of the Native Americans he had seen on his trip out West that summer. Though each of these works was out of place in the student newspaper, one made an impact: A pro-Native American group in Colorado ordered several hundred reprints to distribute to the public.

While at Harvard, Nader was elected president of the *Record* and immediately set out to transform it into an investigative journal. The following year, he wrote an even longer article about Puerto Rico's commonwealth status, and he hoped for the same response that the Native American article had received. The Puerto Rican piece went unnoticed, however, and the staff, along with the school, fell out of love with Nader's ideas about raking muck. Because he wanted the whole newspaper to be slanted toward this type of reportage, but the other newspaper workers and the school did not, Nader resigned his position. However, he did stay on as a senior editor and continued to write muckraking articles of shorter length, alongside the standard student newspaper fare.

Another writer at Harvard at that time was Harold A. Katz, who authored an article for the *Harvard Law Review*—"Liability of Automobile Manufacturers for Unsafe Design of Passenger Cars"—in which he wrote, "Automobile manufacturers have been negligent in failing to design and market reasonably safe automobiles. This failure has created a vast area of unnecessary hazard to human life and is a substantial contributing cause of the high injury and fatality rate in motorcar accidents...Nothing in law or logic insulates manufacturers from liability for deficiencies to design any more than for defects in construction."[16]

Katz insisted that automobile manufacturers should be responsible for making sure that cars work properly and are built properly and that manufacturers should be held accountable for design safety. After studying injuries directly related to design features in cars, he said, "It was apparent that auto manufacturers were marketing millions of cars without any consideration of what was happening to the passengers in accidents. I viewed the carnage as a public health problem."[17] Katz was the first person to suggest that although the drivers were responsible for automobile accidents, design flaws often held equal accountability.

Because he wanted to learn more, Nader called Katz to hear more about the problem. "The purposes of Nader's call to me right after my article was published in the *Review* was to invite me to do an article for his newspaper on other aspects or comments on the same subject. Time considerations prevented me from doing this. Nader was obviously excited about the content of my article. I did not have the impression that he had ever thought about the subject prior to reading my article."[18] Katz followed up his initial article with "The Liability in Tort or Warranty of Automobile Manufacturers for the Inherently Dangerous Design of Passenger Automobiles" in the *Chicago Bar Record* in May 1956.

In his last year of law school, auto safety became Nader's main course of study. He took a course that explored the convergence of law and medicine and wrote his final paper on auto safety liability, entitled "Automotive Design Safety and Legal Liability." He researched the topic doggedly and received a well-deserved A for his effort.

MAKING PRACTICAL CHOICES

After graduating from Harvard, Nader was offered a position clerking for a judge in Alaska. In 1958, the military draft was still in operation, so rather than be drafted, because draft meant a longer term of service under less suitable conditions, Nader joined the Army and spent six months in the Army Reserve at Fort Dix, New Jersey. He went through basic training and then became a cook, where he made soup for thousands of men. He quipped, "If you fell into [a vat], and you didn't know how to swim, you were minestrone."[19]

At the end of his stay at Fort Dix, ever-practical Nader went to the Army Post Exchange (PX) and bought himself a dozen pairs of shoes for $72.00 and four dozen pairs of socks for $16.80 so he should be spared the expense of socks and shoes for years to come. His discharge papers listed "chef" as his comparable occupation.

Nader would never become a chef or a lawyer with his own practice. Although he did open a small law office in Hartford, Connecticut, he never took a case. He was busy traveling and writing.

In April 1959, Nader traveled to Cuba and was party to a press conference held by the new leader of that country—Fidel Castro. "When I interviewed him in April of '59, the U.S. hadn't broken with Cuba yet. In a subsequent interview years later, I found Castro to have great command of detail, and an enormous command of historic detail. He studied all kinds of military histories, going back hundred of years. Everybody who interviewed him says he has a mind for details, figures, and statistics. He works through an interpreter, who is like an alter ego. She's extremely good and very quick, but I'm told that he does understand more English than he admits to."[20]

Nader also traveled to Scandinavia to learn more about ombudsmen (people who investigate citizens' claims and complaints against the government) in the summer of 1961, and then spent some time in Communist-controlled Russia, where he lamented the lack of spontaneity in life. He also traveled to Latin America and wrote articles for *Atlantic Monthly* and *Christian Science Monitor* in 1963, for which he received about $30 an article. Often, these stories were written in airports with a portable typewriter on his lap. He also carried shopping bags stuffed with magazines, documents, and pamphlets that he wanted to read from the various countries that he visited. He also took a pleasure trip to Africa.

Between trips, he worked for the law firm of George Athanson in Hartford, making $75 a week to work with auto accident cases, divorces, and wills. He also lectured at the University of Hartford on government and history. He even spent some time trying to convince Connecticut legislators to sponsor a bill to require safety equipment in cars registered in the state.

His travels became fewer when he got a call from Assistant Labor Secretary Daniel P. Moynihan. Nader had become acquainted with Moynihan some years earlier when he read Moynihan's article "Epidemic on the Highways" in *Reporter* magazine in 1959. Moynihan became known as the first politician in the United States to address auto safety. Nader read the article with interest because he had been writing about the lack of safety features in American cars himself, and though he did not know it at the time, the call from Moynihan signaled a dramatic and propelling change of life.

NOTES

1. Rose B. Nader and Nathra Nader, *It Happened in the Kitchen. Recipes for Food and Thought* (Washington, D.C.: Center for Study of Responsive Law, 1991), p. 16.

2. Quoted in Charles McCarry, *Citizen Nader* (New York: Saturday Review Press, 1972), p. 38.

3. Nader and Nader, *It Happened in the Kitchen. Recipes for Food and Thought*, p. 20.

4. Professor Laura Nader, interview with the author, 7 October 2003.

5. Quoted in Justin Martin, *Nader, Crusader, Spoiler, Icon* (New York: Perseus, 2002), p. 10.

6. Nader and Nader, *It Happened in the Kitchen. Recipes for Food and Thought,* p. 21.

7. Quoted in Martin, *Nader, Crusader, Spoiler, Icon,* p. 11.

8. Quoted in McCarry, *Citizen Nader,* p. 36.

9. "Philosophy of the Gilbert School," *The Gilbert School,* http://www.gilbertschool.org/academics.html.

10. Ralph de Toledano, *Hit & Run, the Rise—And Fall?—of Ralph Nader* (New Rochelle, NY: Arlington House, 1975), p. 28.

11. Professor Laura Nader, interview with the author, 7 October 2003.

12. Those born between 1925 and 1942 and considered to be adaptive as a group.

13. Quoted in McCarry, *Citizen Nader,* p. 45.

14. Quoted in McCarry, *Citizen Nader,* p. 49.

15. Professor Laura Nader, interview with the author, 7 October 2003.

16. Harold A. Katz, "Liability of Automobile Manufacturers for Unsafe Design of Passenger Cars," *Harvard Law Review,* March 1956, p. 864.

17. Harold A. Katz, interview with the author, 5 September 2003.

18. Katz, interview with the author, 5 September 2003.

19. Quoted in Martin, *Nader, Crusader, Spoiler, Icon,* p. 32.

20. Ralph Nader, interview with the author, 15 August 2003.

Chapter 2

UNDER SURVEILLANCE AND IN THE PUBLIC EYE

On April 11, 1959, Ralph Nader's article, "The Safe Car You Can't Buy," was published in *The Nation* magazine and focused on the shortcomings of the safety of American car design. Nader wrote, "It is clear that Detroit today is designing automobiles for style, cost, performance, and calculated obsolescence, but not—despite the 5,000,000 reported accidents, nearly 40,000 fatalities, 110,000 permanent disabilities and 1,500,000 injuries yearly—for safety."[1]

This article was actually published 21 days earlier than the article published by Daniel P. Moynihan, and both men's ideas were similar in nature. Both saw the necessity for manufacturers to consider their customers' safety when designing cars. They advocated what Harold A. Katz had first reported—injury and death were not solely the product of human driving error, but were often caused by poor vehicle design.

Moynihan saw auto safety as the country's biggest public health dilemma. When he became assistant secretary of Labor, under Secretary Arthur Goldberg of the Kennedy administration, he saw a way to bring the issue of auto safety into the Department of Labor with him. Continuing the White House Conference on Traffic Safety, which was instituted in 1954, during the Eisenhower administration, the White House added cabinet members from Labor, Commerce, Defense, and Health, Education, and Welfare. Moynihan served as Goldberg's liaison to the committee, which produced no positive results.

In 1964, Moynihan asked Nader if he would be interested in a job as a consultant on his planning staff, regarding the issue of auto safety, at the pay rate of $50 a day. Nader accepted and was charged with writing a report on the subject. He left his conventional law practice and hitchhiked to Washington, D.C., with one suitcase in his possession.

FINDING HIS NICHE

Moynihan and Nader were very different men. Moynihan was the product of a broken home, a man who liked the taste of drink and intellectual conversation, whereas Nader's own roots were quite stable, his sense of duty and responsibility superseded all else, and he could at times, seem devoid of sentiment. Moynihan, on the other hand, had said after the assassination of President John F. Kennedy, "I don't think there's any point in being Irish if you don't know that the world is going to break your heart eventually."[2]

Yet, their dissimilarities did not alter their relationship. They were not often together because Nader kept erratic hours. He often worked late into the night in the deserted building; he had passion for his assignment. When co-workers were present, he talked nothing but auto safety, and his desk was piled with mounds of papers and files. Only Moynihan knew anything of his progress.

Nader's final product, "A Report of the Context, Condition and Recommended Direction of Federal Activity in Highway Safety," was completed in the spring of 1965. He would have had the report sooner, but he lost his research notes in a taxi at one point and had to reconstruct his data before continuing. At 234 double-spaced pages with 99 pages of notes, Nader's report was thorough and groundbreaking. The auto industry had never been attacked from Nader's angle, and this sparked political interest. In the report's conclusion, Nader urged that the president create a federal highway transportation agency as a separate entity of the government, which would be directly responsible to the president. Later, with some alterations to Nader's plan, this became a reality. The report also recommended that the Treasury create a tax-exempt foundation to determine if and how the auto industry influenced legislation and that the Justice Department become involved in investigating the auto industry for antitrust violations. Nader's report, although outrageous for its time, held information that forced Congress to wake up and listen.

Although the report was not widely distributed to Washington officials, it was solid backup for what Moynihan had in mind. He wanted legislation to regulate the auto industry and to bring focus to the automobile manufacturing defects that were the secondary cause of injury to crash victims.

Much discussion of regulating the auto industry was buzzing on Capitol Hill when Nader was still working on his report. Other matters were also brewing for him, personally. In the summer of 1964, publisher Richard Grossman approached Nader requesting Nader write a book about auto safety. At the time, Grossman had been publishing for about two years, after leaving his position as vice president at Simon & Schuster. His business was small, as it only published about eight books a year, but he was dedicated to publishing only well-written, important books. After reading James Ridgeway's article, "The Corvair Tragedy," in the *New Republic*, Grossman had set his sights on a work on auto safety.

BECOMING AN AUTHOR

Grossman first went to Ridgeway and asked him to write the book, but at the time Ridgeway was overwhelmed with writing commitments. Ridgeway directed Grossman to Nader, who had provided much information on auto safety for Ridgeway's Corvair article.

Grossman tracked Nader down and called him at his rooming house. Nader quickly agreed to do the book. They met at the office of Grossman Publishing, which was a basement apartment at the time, and hammered out a contract agreeing to a $1,500 advance for Nader.

After finishing the report for Moynihan, Nader went to work on his book, for which he had already laid much of the groundwork. He also continued his research with documents from the California Highway Department, which identified car models that had unusually high rates of accidents. He also used depositions from lawsuits against auto manufacturers, patent filings, and articles in the GM *Engineering Journal*.

His best source of information came from disgruntled employees from the auto industry, and he referenced the work of auto safety pioneers, such as William Haddon Jr. and Hugh DeHaven, who felt that people could better survive auto crashes if they were protected from what Highway Patrolman Elmer Paul termed the "second collision"—when passengers are injured by components inside the vehicle, such as the tragedy Nader had witnessed when the child was nearly decapitated by the open glove compartment door.

At that time, manufacturers felt that shiny chrome caught buyers' attention and so, made dashboards from metal. That hard surface plus the lack of seatbelts and glove compartments that were situated too high on the dashboard, too tinny, and poised to pop open on impact created some dangerous elements inside the family automobile. When passengers flew around inside the vehicle on impact, they were often injured or killed by defects in the car's design, rather than by the collision itself.

Haddon had studied both engineering and medicine, which gave him an advantage in studying auto safety. He believed that greater safety in interior engineering would save lives. Nader's article "Epidemic on the Highways" was Nader's attempt to bring these ideas to the public. He had no idea that he would be doing so in a much more important way. Senator Abraham A. Ribicoff of Connecticut was about to make Nader and his cause famous.

TESTIFYING BEFORE CONGRESS

Ribicoff was the secretary of Health, Education, and Welfare during the John F. Kennedy administration. Ribicoff then served as governor of Connecticut. He was elected as U.S. Senator in 1962. In 1965, Ribicoff was chairman of the Subcommittee on Executive Reorganization of the Committee on Government Operations. In essence, his job was to find issues that would interest other senators. Early that year, he decided to study auto safety. He had begun to look into the issue while still governor of Connecticut, and he charged staff director and general counsel for the Senate subcommittee, Jerome Sonosky, with finding expert witnesses. After meeting Nader, Sonosky phoned Ribicoff and exclaimed, "We just struck gold!"[3] Nader was the ultimate expert on auto safety, and they made him an unpaid advisor to Ribicoff's subcommittee.

During this period of study and fact gathering, Nader had a hard time concentrating on writing his book. Grossman had wanted to publish the title on Memorial Day or Labor Day to coincide with holidays famous for heavy highway traffic accidents. Nader missed both. Ultimately, Grossman had to go to Washington, D.C., to see that the work was completed. He knew it would be an important book and was determined to see it through, so he and Nader sat side by side, typing away. The moment Nader finished a page, Grossman edited it. Finally, after 22 days of intensive, nonstop writing and editing, the work was finished.

Eleven thousand copies of *Unsafe at Any Speed, the Designed-In Dangers of the American Automobile* were ready on November 30, 1965. Although the book showed the manufacturers' responsibility to protect its customers by designing more people-friendly products, it also focused on Nader's icon of dangerous automobiles—the Chevrolet Corvair.

In the late 1950s, car manufacturers became concerned about meeting the competition with smaller import cars, especially with the original

Volkswagen Beetle, which had come into the states after World War II and had become very popular. For the 1960 models, introduced in 1959, the "Big Three" (General Motors [GM], Ford, and Chrysler) came out with their own small cars—the Chevrolet Corvair, the Ford Falcon, and the Plymouth Valiant, which had a cousin, the Dodge Dart.

Yet, the Corvair was different from the other American cars. Like the Volkswagen, the Corvair's aluminum air-cooled engine, called a pancake six, was in the back, and the trunk was in the front. Chevrolet also touted the Corvair's frameless construction, independent suspension at every wheel, flatter floor, and a fold-down rear seat. GM's 1960 Corvair brochure read, "America's only compact car that isn't just a small echo of a big one." This statement pointed to their innovative new product and hinted that Ford and Chrysler were just shrinking their larger models.

People loved the Corvair for these modern features, and before 1964, about one million had been sold. Yet Nader titled his first chapter in *Unsafe at Any Speed*, "The Sporty Corvair: The 'One-Car' Accident." His basis for landing on the Corvair in particular was that by 1965, one hundred damage suits had been filed involving that particular model, but GM continually blamed driver negligence for the accidents involving their beloved design.

Nader cited an engineering flaw—the Corvair's swing-axle independent rear suspension. In *Unsafe at Any Speed*, Nader quoted a California auto specialist, who detailed the problem: "With the Corvair's center of gravity and high roll couple of the suspension, body lean becomes a considerable force acting to tuck both wheels under in a cornering attitude. This results in loss of adhesion because of lowered tire surface contact. The sudden breakaway which has been experienced by every Corvair driver comes when a slight irregularity in the surface destroys the small amount of adhesion remaining."[4]

Expressly, when a driver tried to corner too fast, the wheels tucked under and tended to make the car roll. This was especially true when the road surface was not even. This problem was alleviated when in 1964, Chevrolet added an anti-sway bar between the Corvair's front wheels and a single-leaf transverse spring under the rear end to help keep the wheels on the ground, lower the roll center, and correct oversteer, among other benefits. In 1965, Chevrolet eliminated the swing axles entirely, which prevented the car from changing camber on an uneven surface.

Yet, Nader knew there were hundreds of thousands of Corvairs still on the road with serious problems, and though his book shows significant disregard for passengers in Ford and Chrysler vehicles, as well, the Corvair seemed to take the brunt of his eye-opening revelations. *Unsafe at Any Speed* was published in November 1965; in December, registrations for the Chevrolet Corvair dropped 42 percent from the same month the year before.

NADER AND GM

Nader went after GM in particular partly because of the Corvair, but also because of a 1949 lawsuit in which GM was convicted of criminally conspiring to rip up tracks for inner-city rail systems (streetcars) all over the country, to monopolize the sale of buses to transportation companies. Also involved in this action were Standard Oil of California, Firestone, and other companies that would certainly benefit because of the rail system destruction. The convicted companies were fined a mere $5,000 each. Some call this the corporate crime of the century.

GM executives, not wanting another barrage of bad publicity for the corporation, were not happy with Nader's book and his treatment of the Corvair and assumed that he was working in league with those in litigation regarding the car. GM Chairman Frederic G. Donner and GM Chairman and CEO James M. Roche had already appeared before Ribicoff's senate subcommittee in July, and the senators were less than gentle with their questions:

> Senator Robert Kennedy:...You made $1.7 billion last year?
>
> Mr. Donner: That is correct.
>
> Senator Kennedy: And you spent $1 million on [safety research]?
>
> Mr. Donner: In this particular facet we are talking about...
>
> Senator Kennedy: If you gave just one percent of your profits, that would be $17 million.[5]

So much was going badly for GM, the company hoped to neutralize Nader, and it was quietly decided to start an investigation with the hope of finding something lacking in his character. Nader first began to suspect he was under surveillance in Iowa, on January 7, 1966. At the invitation of Iowa's Attorney General Lawrence Scalise, Nader was in Des Moines to testify at a series of hearings before public officials. The day before, a press conference had been held at the Sheraton Cadillac Hotel in Detroit for *Unsafe at Any Speed*. Executives from all the big auto companies had been invited to attend to debate Nader on his findings. Not one representative from any company appeared.

GM issued a statement through GM Vice President Louis B. Goud, assistant to Roche. Goud said, "We do not agree with the conclusions drawn by Mr. Nader and can see no point in engaging in a discussion with him concerning these conclusions at a press conference."[6] Yet, GM executives also invited Nader to discuss engineering issues with employees at the GM Technical Center in Warren, Michigan. Nader had already been there and had taken the tour several times. He concluded that only vague information was disclosed at these meetings, everything else was private.

In his Iowa testimony the following day, Nader pointed out the arrogance of GM's actions and said, "What reasons could there be for auto makers, who have taken literally billions of dollars out of the State of Iowa through the sales of their trucks and automobiles, not to…appear in person and answer questions pertaining to the hundreds of deaths and thousands of injuries, which occur yearly in this state involving the operation of those products which they sell."[7]

Nader stated in his book that 47,700 people had been killed and four million had been injured as a result of auto accidents in 1964 alone, meaning that in 1964, one out of every two Americans were potential auto crash victims, and he placed the blame squarely on bad engineering. He was outraged that automotive manufacturers were ignoring the problem completely.

UNDER WATCHFUL EYES

Several times while in residence at the Kirkwood Hotel in Des Moines, Iowa, Nader had noticed men who seemed to be hovering near him. People thought him paranoid in the past. He once told Moynihan to be careful, that the phone might be bugged, and was gently rebuffed. But this time was different.

Nader had seen a man twice on the first floor and once outside his room, and the man's presence gave Nader an eerie feeling, as if he was being tracked. Nader informed Scalise of his suspicions, and Scalise took Nader seriously. Scalise ordered an investigation for harassment of a witness, but by the time the inquiry got underway, the action was futile and the investigation was dropped.

On January 14, while Nader took GM up on its offer to visit the Technical Center again, Senator Ribicoff announced a new round of hearings on auto safety, beginning in February, for which Nader would be a principal witness. The date was set for February 10.

For several days beforehand, Nader received several crank calls. Nader lived in a $50 a month rooming house, so he used a pay telephone on the wall to accept and receive calls, and few people had his number. Typically, Nader would go to the phone and when he answered, the caller would hang up. Some calls were more intimidating in tone. "You are fighting a losing battle," or "Why don't you change your field of interest?"[8] were two warnings. Another call told him to pick up a package at Railway Express and then hung up. The final call on February 9, the night before his scheduled testimony was, "Why don't you go back to Connecticut, buddy boy?,"[9] followed by a dial tone.

The following day, Nader appeared in Room 318 of the Dirksen Senate Office Building to provide testimony before the Senate subcommittee. In addition to Ribicoff and Kennedy, members included Senators Jacob Javitz of New York, Carl Curtis of Nebraska, Gaylord Nelson of Wisconsin, and Vance Hartke of Indiana. Senator Walter Mondale of Minnesota was also a member of the committee, but was not often present because he was getting ready to run as the Democratic presidential candidate in 1968.

Nader's testimony was self-assured and calmly presented. At one point, he denigrated the violence with which car makers tag their vehicles and said, "Ford continues to name its cars with such aggressive and ferocious titles as Comet, Meteor, Thunderbird, Cobra, Mustang (Mustang means 'a wild unbreakable horse'), and Marauder (which means literally 'one who pillages and lays waste to the countryside')."[10] In this first foray into public prominence, Nader showed the courage of his convictions and his alacrity with producing solid facts to prove his points.

The next day, Nader returned to the Senate Office Building for an interview with NBC television. Just after he went into the pressroom, two men showed up and asked the security guard at the desk where Nader had gone, telling the guard they were detectives. When the security guard told Sonosky of this, Sonosky was amazed. Nader had confided his suspicions that he was being followed to Sonosky, who told Nader to stop being paranoid. Now, there was proof. Sonosky immediately called Ribicoff and disclosed the incident. Ribicoff ordered an investigation, citing harassment of a congressional witness.

The news broke in the *Washington Post* the following Sunday. "This was disclosed by Nader yesterday and supported by Bryce Nelson, a *Washington Post* reporter who inadvertently became involved in the bizarre episode when he was mistaken for Nader."[11] Although the article was unsigned, Morton Mintz, who later became a crucial element in Nader's success, had written it. Nader had selected Mintz to divulge this story because of the Pulitzer Prize–winning stories Mintz had published regarding the drug thalidomide, which had been prescribed for pregnant women experiencing morning sickness and was later found to cause birth defects. Because of Mintz's "muckraking," Nader thought Mintz would be receptive. Mintz's story, "Car Safety Critic Nader Reports Being 'Tailed,'" appeared in the February 13, 1966 edition of the *Washington Post*.

THE INVESTIGATION PERSISTS

The report did not seem to faze the investigators because they stepped up their harassment. Nader realized this when he received a call from one of his old law professors at Harvard, congratulating him on his new job. There was no new job. Nader's professor said that he had been contacted for a reference, but Nader had no idea about the episode beforehand. On another occasion, as Nader stood reading an automotive magazine in a drug store, a young woman approached him and asked him to join a discussion group on foreign affairs. She said they were looking for new members. Nader declined. Then, in a grocery store, he was approached by another young woman who asked him to help her move some furniture. Nader apologized, saying he was running late, and the woman left the store without asking another man to help her. These instances were strange and so close together that Nader began to realize that whoever was investigating him was trying to set him up in an awkward situation with a woman.

A bit of concrete evidence surfaced when Nader received a telephone call from Frederick Condon, a friend from Harvard, who had become paraplegic because of an auto accident. (Nader dedicated *Unsafe at Any Speed* to Condon.) Condon said that he had received a call from a Mr. Warren, who said he was investigating Nader's background for a client who was interested in hiring Nader for a researcher's position. Warren informed Condon that his questions would involve information about Nader's work background, his sex life, and his politics.

Preemployment screening is not usually that intrusive, so Condon began to suspect something was up. He asked "Mr. Warren" who he was working for, but Warren would not disclose his employer, except to say that he was working for "Mr. Gillen." To assess the situation more fully, Condon invited Warren to his office that afternoon.

When Warren arrived, he then addressed himself as Mr. Gillen. Condon was sure the two men were the same person because he recognized the man's voice. Gillen was fiftyish with graying hair and black horn-rimmed glasses. He sat holding his briefcase on his lap, which caused Condon to suspect that Gillen was taping the conversation. Gillen began with questions regarding Nader's driving record. Then, Gillen went into Nader's personal life, suggesting that it was unusual for a man of Nader's age not to have been married and hinting that he wanted to verify that Nader was not homosexual. Gillen also inquired about Nader's Arabic roots, wondering whether Nader was anti-Semitic. When the interview was over, Condon wrote about what had happened while his memory was fresh. He then called Nader.

Nader contacted Ridgeway at the *New Republic* and gave him contact information for the people who had been interviewed regarding Nader's so-called employment check. Ridgeway developed the story and uncovered Vincent Gillen of Vincent Gillen Associates in Garden City, New York—a detective agency. When Ridgeway spoke with Gillen, Gillen still would not divulge his employer, saying only that Nader was being considered for an important job.

When Ridgeway's story hit the stands on March 4, 1966, a media frenzy ignited, and several of the big auto companies, including Chrysler, Ford, and American Motors officially denied they had been involved in any way. GM made no remarks. Because Nader had investigated GM's Corvair in particular, the press took GM's silence as affirmation and descended on the giant company.

On March 9, 1966, GM issued a press release stating that its office of general counsel had initiated the investigation to determine whether Nader was acting on behalf of the people who had filed lawsuits against GM for injuries sustained while riding in Corvairs.

THE TABLES TURN

Ribicoff was furious when the statement was made public. Although GM claimed that the investigation was "routine," Nader was a congressional witness and harassment of such an individual is a federal crime. Ribicoff immediately called a hearing for March 22, and Nader was asked to attend, along with Roche and Gillen. The FBI also announced plans to enter the case.

On the day of the hearing, the Caucus Room of the Old Senate Office Building was packed with reporters and spectators. Ribicoff opened the hearing by stating that the expert witnesses who had testified before the committee had been of tremendous help in drafting the national highway safety bill, which had recently been forwarded to Congress by the president. Ribicoff also asserted a witness's right to testify truthfully without fear of reprisal. He announced that the current session would investigate the attempt by GM to discredit Nader.

Nader was the first witness to be called, but he was not in the building. The committee recessed for 15 minutes, but when Nader still had not arrived, Ribicoff asked Roche to present his testimony under oath.

As a political ploy, Roche had enlisted the services of Theodore (Ted) Sorenson as his general counsel for the hearing. Sorenson had been speechwriter, friend, and consultant to President Kennedy during the previous administration, and because Sorenson knew most of the senators on the subcommittee, Roche tried to lend an "Old Boy" air to the proceedings. However, the ploy backfired when the committee immediately saw the attempt to make the hearing more "buddy" oriented. Ribicoff decided that the situation would require more toughness, lest the hearing be considered trivial.

After looking over the case, Sorenson had no solutions for GM. His only advice to Roche was to stand up and apologize, so the sixtyish, white-haired Roche stood and said, "To the extent that General Motors bears responsibility, I want to apologize here and now to the members of this subcommittee and Mr. Nader. I sincerely hope that these apologies will be accepted. Certainly I bear Mr. Nader no ill will."[12]

Roche continued his comments by insisting that GM's investigation was only to prove that Nader was not working on behalf of the litigants suing GM over the Corvair's faulty design, while writing books and articles regarding the automobile's inefficacy. To do so would have been a violation of the Canons of Professional Ethics of the American Bar Association, which state, in part, "Newspaper publications by a lawyer as to pending or anticipated litigation may interfere with a fair trial in the Courts and otherwise prejudice the due administration of justice."[13] Roche went on to declare no personal knowledge of the investigation and said that if issues other than Nader's ethics were discussed in the process, these questions were not asked at his request.

After the statement, Senators Ribicoff, Kennedy, and Milward L. Simpson (of Wyoming) all commended Roche on the forthrightness of his statement. The committee had more questions, however. First, Senator Kennedy questioned Roche on the validity of the statement initially delivered to the public by GM on March 9. Roche had to admit that the statement regarding the company's uninvolvement was too broad and that Roche's preceding testimony had negated the disclaimer of harassment.

Senator Fred R. Harris of Oklahoma then took over the questioning and tried to determine who had ordered the investigation of Nader's personal life. "Who made the decision that extraneous matters be investigated?" Harris asked.[14] To which Roche replied, "I think that the decision was made by the people who were conducting the investigation."[15] Roche went on to verify that no one in the employ of GM had ordered such information.

Senator Kennedy spoke up again. In an advance copy of testimony to be presented later in the proceedings, he cited a passage claiming that a woman on GM's legal staff ordered an investigation from the Washington law firm of Alvord & Alvord, and in a conversation with one of their attorneys gave the type of information they wanted collected, which included Nader's sources of income, the location of his law practice, a list of his business associates, a description of his movements, and in short, "a complete background investigation of Mr. Nader's activities."[16] Roche claimed no knowledge of this order at the time of the March 9 statement release.

MORE DAMNING EVIDENCE

Other witnesses were interviewed during the proceedings, but none was so detrimental to GM as was Gillen. He opened his statement by rattling off experience relevant to his expertise in the field of surveillance: special agent for the FBI, lawyer, insurance company investigator, employment investigator, and licensed private detective. He then denied ever trailing Nader in Iowa, but did admit that his men were the ones who followed Nader into the New Senate Office Building on February 11. However, he did deny the allegations that his men had spoken to the security guard there or that they had ever followed a *Washington Post* reporter in error. Gillen explained that they used the preemployment investigation ruse so that people would not think Nader had done anything wrong. He said that in connection with such an investigation, personal questions are routine and that to keep up the ruse, those questions had to be asked so that interview subjects would continue to think their questions pertained to employment.

Senator Kennedy then said, "What you mean [is] that you were conducting the investigation under a lie and that you had to carry out the lie completely."[17] Gillen continued to insist that he was just doing his job and that he had not harassed Nader.

Then, came Nader—the witness the entire courtroom had shown up to see. He started his testimony by apologizing for being late. He had left home early, but had been unable to get a cab into the city. He said, "I almost felt like going out and buying a Chevrolet,"[18] which broke the tension in the room with a few snickers. Then, he went on to give his formal statement. Nader adamantly declared that he was not involved in any Corvair litigation brought by individuals and said that he was interested in tort law (law that allows injured parties to obtain compensation from any entity that causes the injury) surrounding the Corvair, but was not involved in any personal proceedings. He said that GM's suspicions that his motivations were about continuing litigation were not his problem. "They simply cannot understand that the prevention of cruelty to humans can be a sufficient motivation for one endeavoring to obtain the manufacture of safer cars."[19] He also suggested that corporate executives who delivered substandard products to the public should be criminally prosecuted.

The committee praised Nader for his willingness to go after the corporate giants and for his courage and integrity. Ribicoff also commented that it was commendable that a $6,700 investigation (approximately $37,000 in 2003) turned up nothing negative in Nader's background.

Following his Capitol Hill testimony, Nader was a celebrity. *Unsafe at Any Speed* went to the top of the bestseller lists and the entire mêlée over his investigation had strengthened the public's sentiment about auto safety. The week of May 15, 1966, was proclaimed as "National Transportation Week" by President Lyndon B. Johnson, who also signed new legislation on September 9, creating the National Highway Safety Bureau and naming William Haddon Jr. as its head.

Although GM had not been prosecuted for harassing a congressional witness, Nader filed suit against the company on November 14, 1966, charging invasion of privacy, and asking for damages of $26 million.

NOTES

1. Ralph Nader, "The Ralph Nader Reader," *The Nation*, 11 April, 1959, (reprint, New York: Seven Stories Press, 2000), p. 267.

2. Ambassador Robert D. Blackwill, "Tribute to Senator Daniel Patrick Moynihan," United States Consulate, Mumbai, India, 27 March 2003, http://usembassy.state.gov/mumbai/wwwhwashnews224.html.

3. Quoted in Justin Martin, *Nader, Crusader, Spoiler, Icon* (New York: Perseus, 2002), p. 44.

4. Ralph Nader, *Unsafe at Any Speed, the Designed-In Dangers of the American Automobile* (New York: Grossman, 1965; reprint, New York: Pocket Books, 1966), p. 10 (reprint ed.).

5. Quoted in Thomas Whiteside, *The Investigation of Ralph Nader, General Motors vs. One Determined Man* (New York: Arbor House, 1972; reprint, New York: Pocket Books, 1972), p. 6 (reprint ed.).

6. Quoted in Whiteside, *The Investigation of Ralph Nader, General Motors vs. One Determined Man*, p. 11.

7. Quoted in Whiteside, *The Investigation of Ralph Nader, General Motors vs. One Determined Man*, p. 13.

8. Quoted in Whiteside, *The Investigation of Ralph Nader, General Motors vs. One Determined Man*, p. 18.

9. Quoted in Whiteside, *The Investigation of Ralph Nader, General Motors vs. One Determined Man*, p. 18.

10. Quoted in Martin, *Nader, Crusader, Spoiler, Icon*, p. 48.

11. Quoted in Whiteside, *The Investigation of Ralph Nader, General Motors vs. One Determined Man*, p. 21.

12. Quoted in Whiteside, *The Investigation of Ralph Nader, General Motors vs. One Determined Man*, p. 39.

13. Quoted in *Gentile v. State Bar of Nevada*, 501 U.S. 1030 (1991).

14. Quoted in Whiteside, *The Investigation of Ralph Nader, General Motors vs. One Determined Man*, p. 47.

15. Quoted in Whiteside, *The Investigation of Ralph Nader, General Motors vs. One Determined Man*, p. 47.

16. Quoted in Whiteside, *The Investigation of Ralph Nader, General Motors vs. One Determined Man*, p. 48.

17. Quoted in Whiteside, *The Investigation of Ralph Nader, General Motors vs. One Determined Man*, p. 82.

18. Quoted in Martin, *Nader, Crusader, Spoiler, Icon*, p. 58.

19. Quoted in Martin, *Nader, Crusader, Spoiler, Icon*, p. 53.

Chapter 3

BIG BUSINESS ON THE HOT SEAT

Through his victory over General Motors (GM), Ralph Nader had effectively created a market for the type of law he had wanted to practice all along—legal advocacy for the public. He terms it responsive law, and his interest had its roots in the work of Roscoe Pound, who is often termed the father of sociological jurisprudence.

This form of law challenges the mores of the times—why is one law enforced but not another and what laws are relevant from generation to generation? For instance, prohibition of alcohol was legislated in the 1920s because of public outcry over the high level of alcoholic consumption among the American population. By 1933, the legislation was repealed when illegal stores of alcohol became rampant, and the population had decided to ignore the law. The masses had voted to accept alcohol through their actions alone. The duty of justices to consider these sociological changes when developing an interpretation of the law is the gist of sociological jurisprudence.

Roscoe Pound had been one of Nader's mentors at Harvard. At the time, Pound was in his eighties. Although he had been the dean of Harvard Law School from 1916 to 1936, he was by Nader's time dean emeritus, an honorary title meaning that he had been dean before retiring. Pound was still a prolific writer and scholar, and he retained a small office at the school.

Nader saw Pound walking through one of the campus buildings one day and realized how students and the administration viewed him—as an anachronism. Nader began a friendship with Pound and often asked Pound for reprints of articles he had written. Pound influenced Nader, who found him so inspiring he once asked Pound if he could write his biography. Pound declined, musing that he might write an autobiography one day. He never did before his death in 1964.

Along with the experiences with Pound, Nader also studied the ombudsman system in Scandinavia with great interest and had decided that rather than a private law practice, which would have been much more lucrative, he wanted to champion the interest of average consumers, never mind the personal costs. In 1966, the nation was prime for such action, and Nader was in the right place. By the end of that year, he was seen as the person most likely to succeed at challenging the corporations.

In 1967, the Vietnam War had begun to heat up in Southeast Asia as U.S. bombs struck Hanoi. In what they termed The Summer of Love, the hippies, who opposed traditional middle-class lifestyles, held their first Human Be-in in Golden Gate Park in San Francisco, where more than 25,000 people listened to such 1960s legends as LSD proponent Dr. Timothy Leary, poet Allen Ginsberg, and rock bands like the Grateful Dead and Jefferson Airplane. In all parts of the country, Americans of all ages protested the draft of young men into the armed forces and the war in Vietnam. Awareness of the impact of politics on human life was taking center stage.

CONSUMERISM, WATCHWORD OF THE DAY

Nader was sometimes criticized because his issues were not those of his activist cohorts. Rather than demonstrate against the war, rally for civil rights, or embrace the soon-to-be emerging women's movement, Nader preferred to work within the legislative system on issues where he could save more human lives because the number of people killed in Vietnam was far less than those killed on highways, and those fatalities included women and children. He also pointed out that the very issues he was involved in fighting for consumers were related to those people living in poverty and the urban ghetto. He did not work directly for civil rights because he saw that many people already working on those issues had more political power.

President Lyndon B. Johnson's administration was known for its progressive stance on Civil Rights, but Johnson was on the consumer rights bandwagon as well. On February 16, he sent a special message to Congress. Among other issues, his request called for "truth in lending," so that lenders would disclose annual percentage rates and other important aspects of every loan made in the United States; more stringent meat inspection regulations to include the 15 percent of meat packers not regulated by federal inspectors; and creation of the National Commission on Product Safety. "Consumerism" became the watchword of the day, and Nader took the banner and ran with it.

Nader was not the first consumer activist in American history. In the late nineteenth century, conditions in the United States were not nearly as sanitary as they are today. Milk was still not pasteurized, and ice was the only means of refrigeration. Many patent medicines, such as "Kick-a-poo Indian Sagwa" and "Warner's Safe Cure for Diabetes," were still on the market, and they often contained cocaine, opium, morphine, or even heroin. They were usually sold without labeling or distinction, and when labels did exist, the patent medicines claimed to cure diseases that even modern medicine cannot control. Although some firms were producing good products, Dr. Harvey Wiley, who was the sixth head of the U.S. Department of Agriculture's Division of Chemistry in 1883, put his chemists on projects that would protect the public from such abuses and used publicity to promote his cause.

In 1903, Wiley established a group of volunteers who agreed to eat foods treated with chemical preservatives to learn the consequences to their health, if any. They were called the "poison squad." A song was even written about them, with the chorus as follows:

"O, they may get over it but they'll never look the same,

That kind of bill of fare would drive most men insane.

Next week he will give them mothballs, á la Newburgh or else plain;

O, they may get over it but they'll never look the same.[1]

Although the public rallied for Wiley's campaign for a federal food and drug law, patent medicine firms and whiskey distillers were against him, and argued that it was no business of the federal government what people ate or drank. But the women's clubs of America became strong supporters of Wiley, and with their added campaigning for Wiley's reforms, the 1906 Food and Drug Act, also establishing the regulatory agency the Food and Drug Administration, was finally passed on June 30, 1906.

Other early activists include Frederick Schlink and Stuart Chase, who in 1927 wrote the book *Your Money's Worth*, which advocated scientific testing of products to uncover deceptions in advertising. In his book *100,000,000 Guinea Pigs: Dangers in Everyday Foods, Drugs and Cosmetics* Arthur Kallet also came out for independent product testing, and Colston Wayne helped found the Consumer's Union in 1930, which to this day publishes *Consumer Reports*, giving consumers accurate and valid information on the products they buy.

Closer to the time Nader was studying auto safety, Rachel Carson published her environmental protection treatise *Silent Spring*, a well-documented testament to the environmental danger and health risks of using pesticides, especially the DDT that Nader had complained about and that killed so many birds when he was at Princeton.

UNSAFE ON ANY FORK

Johnson's letter to Congress brought up the meat packing industry, but Nader was interested in the lack of standards for companies that bought, packaged, and re-sold meat within one state. Yet, neither Johnson nor Nader was the first to bring the abuses in meat packing to the attention of the public.

Upton Sinclair's 1905 novel *The Jungle* exposed corruption in the Chicago meatpacking industry with passages such as the following:

> The people of Chicago saw the government inspectors in Packingtown, and they all took that to mean that they were protected from diseased meat; they did not understand that these hundred and sixty-three inspectors had been appointed at the request of the packers, and that they were paid by the United States government to certify that all the diseased meat was kept in the state. They had no authority beyond that; for the inspection of meat to be sold in the city and state the whole force in Packingtown consisted of three henchmen of the local political machine! And shortly afterward, one of these a physician made the discovery that the carcasses of steers which had been condemned as tubercular by the government inspectors, and which therefore contained ptomaines, which are deadly poisons, were left upon an open platform and carted away to be sold in the city; and so he insisted that these carcasses be treated with an injection of kerosene—and was ordered to resign the same week! So indignant were the packers that they went farther, and compelled the mayor to abolish the whole bureau of inspection; so that since then there has not been even a pretence of any interference with the graft. There was said to be two thousand dollars a week hush money from the tubercular steers alone; and as much again from the hogs which had died of cholera on the trains, and which you might see any day being loaded into boxcars and hauled away to a place called Globe, in Indiana, where they made a fancy grade of lard.[2]

The uproar from Sinclair's book caused meat consumption to decrease dramatically, and the charges upset President Theodore Roosevelt so much that he put muscle behind the languishing Pure Food and Drug Act, which had been heavily lobbied against by the "beef trust," the drug companies, and other food companies. The act Roosevelt signed into legislation in 1906 as the Pure Food and Drug Act included a provision for all foods and drugs destined for human consumption to be tested and inspected by the federal government. To enhance the regulations on meat, the Meat Inspection Act of 1906 furthered protective measures by requiring all cattle, sheep, horses, goats, and swine to be inspected before and after slaughter. It also established standards for cleanliness of the packaging plants.

The Pure Food and Drug Act stated in part

> That the Secretary of the Treasury, the Secretary of Agriculture, and the Secretary of Commerce and Labor shall make uniform rules and regulations for carrying out the provisions of this Act, including the collection and examination of specimens of foods and drugs manufactured or offered for sale in the District of Columbia, or in any Territory of the United States, or which shall be offered for sale in unbroken packages in any State other than that in which they shall have been respectively manufactured or produced, or which shall be received from any foreign country, or intended for shipment to any foreign country, or which may be submitted for examination by the chief health, food, or drug officer of any State, Territory, or the District of Columbia, or at any domestic or foreign port through which such product is offered for interstate commerce, or for export or import between the United States and any foreign port or country."[3]

And therein lies the rub—"which shall be offered for sale in unbroken packages in any State other than that in which they shall have been respectively manufactured or produced, or which shall be received from any foreign country..."[4] Meat was not subject to federal inspection as long as it was not intended for transport across state lines.

FIXING THE LOOPHOLE

This loophole in the law came to the attention of Congressman Neal Smith of Idaho, who studied what happened at livestock auctions and realized that the buyers of diseased cattle and hogs were the same people every time. When he found that these buyers were selling the diseased meat to consumers, yet operating within the existing law, he was adamant about getting the 1906 regulations amended.

Smith's legislative assistant at the time was an old friend of Nader's, and he mentioned the meat dilemma to Nader, who adopted the cause. Nader had worked at his father's restaurant and had helped with ordering meat at times. Nader had also been a cook in the army. The topic appealed to him.

Two articles written by Nader—"Watch That Hamburger" and "We're Still in the Jungle"—appeared in the summer of 1967 in the *New Republic*. He reported that enough meat for 30 million people a year was not adequately inspected and wrote, "Eyeballs, lungs, hog blood and chopped hides and other indelicate carcass portions are blended skillfully into bologna and hot dogs."[5]

Nader's articles gained attention, as did those of Nathan (Nick) Kotz, a contributing writer to the Des Moines *Register* and the Minneapolis *Tribune*. Kotz's work on intrastate meat processing won a Pulitzer Prize 1968, but Nader put the issue right in the public's face. By working with Kotz, Nader obtained data Kotz had gathered, broke the statistics down state by state, and sent press releases to newspapers where the worst meat processing plants were situated. Well-known meat processors, such as Armour and Swift, operated some of these plants, so the newspapers used the information. Nader also went on the road with his campaign to Boston and Los Angeles and wrote letters to former actress and Westinghouse spokesperson Betty Furness, President Johnson's Special Assistant for Consumer Affairs. Following the publicity Nader generated, Furness was inundated with letters from meat inspectors and people all over the country, demanding tougher legislation.

Smith introduced a bill to strengthen the 1906 act in Congress, while Nader continued to gather support, both from the public and from Congress. He also became a regular witness before the agriculture committees in both the House and the Senate and distributed his prepared remarks to newspapers beforehand because he had realized how important it was to keep an issue alive in the press.

On October 31, 1967, the House passed a bill (HR12144) making intrastate meat packers responsible for meeting federal guidelines. Yet, it was a weaker bill than Smith and Nader had intended. The meat packing lobby had successfully pressured congressmen to water down the stronger legislation, which required federal inspection of plants doing more than $250,000 worth of intrastate business a year. The original, stronger bill had been introduced by Smith and Congressman Thomas S. Foley (from the state of Washington) and was narrowly rejected by a 104 to 98 vote. Furness, the American Meat Institute, and meat industry unions had supported the Smith-Foley proposal, while the Western States Meat Packers supported the weaker bill that passed.

Once again, special interest had the greater clout, and the same politics continue. Congress members are usually reluctant to go against the big corporations because the members depend on these giants for campaign contributions and for bringing in votes from their industries during elections.

Sometimes, however, special interests are reigned in more tightly than they would like. On November 28, the Senate strengthened the House's October 31 bill, requiring states to make inspection standards at least comparable to federal standards and gave meat packers a two-year window to bring their operations to par. Yet, it provided an option for a state's governor to waive the two-year grace period. This option did not sit well with the chairman of the House Agriculture Committee and head of the House conferees on the bill nor with Southern Democrats, who saw the intrastate features of the bill as an invasion of states' rights. Finally, when the waiver provision was removed from the legislation, the House conferees accepted the Senate's amendments and the measure passed. President Johnson signed the Wholesome Meat Act of 1967 into law on December 15, with both Nader and 89-year-old Upton Sinclair present for the ceremony. In part, the act reads

> The Secretary is authorized, whenever he determines that it would effectuate the purposes of this chapter, to cooperate with the appropriate State agency in developing and administering a State meat inspection program in any State which has enacted a State meat inspection law that imposes mandatory ante mortem and post mortem inspection, reinspection and sanitation requirements that are at least equal to those under subchapter I of this chapter, with respect to all or certain classes of persons engaged in the State in slaughtering cattle, sheep, swine, goats, or equines, or preparing the carcasses, parts thereof, meat or meat food products, of any such animals for use as human food solely for distribution within such State.[6]

With these words, the federal government became responsible for overseeing intrastate meat inspection and packaging. In the first year of the new regulations, more than 700 meatpacking and processing plants closed. Many closings were voluntary, but states suspended 98 licenses and closed 59 plants. Rosemary Mucklow, executive director of the National Meat Association remarked, "In one big sweep, a host of firms were brought within the statuary arm of the Federal Meat Inspection Act. Many of the firms just never made it—they simply went out of business during the breaking in phase."[7]

SIR RALPH

With this new victory, Nader was less associated with just the automobile industry and was soon classified as an all-around consumer activist. Still, he continued to put pressure on Capitol Hill regarding auto safety. On January 7, 1968, he accused the auto industry of manipulating the president's tacit endorsement of higher automobile prices. He commented that new safety feature regulations, which had taken effect on January 1 of that year, were only an excuse for an exorbitant increase in prices. Nader never let up and the consumers seemed to appreciate his dedication and his Spartan personal lifestyle. He had fashioned himself as a media star in the name of the public good.

The January 22, 1968, cover of *Newsweek* even sported an image of Nader in a suit of armor. The feature behind it was entitled "Meet Ralph Nader." The people were behind him, and he knew how to get things done—through manipulation of the press and persons able to make a difference. Nader's strange work schedule—whereby he slept only four to five hours a day and worked in the middle of the night—spilled over to his allies because he often called them in the wee hours to discuss issues and strategy.

Senator Walter Mondale of Minnesota was instrumental in getting the Wholesome Meat Act approved in the Senate, and Nader fed him a great deal of statistical and other information. Mondale became so used to getting phone calls in the middle of the night from Nader that he would pick up the phone and say, "Hello, Ralph."[8]

Nader knew how to get someone's attention and how to use the press. Usually, he would send a copy of a letter he had written to one official or another to a reporter on Friday. The news is usually slow on weekends, so editors are highly interested in getting meaty content for the slack time; stories about Nader's issues would usually reach the public and the government official at the same time. This meant that the official was on the hot seat to respond immediately to Nader's outrage, though he would not receive the letter until Monday. Nader was not always completely accurate with the facts in his letters, however. Reporters often wondered if he sent things out just to get a reaction. The keystone of his argument is always a call for curative action, and by doing so, he added a moral tone to each issue, which people are reluctant to overlook.

During 1968, Nader used his ability to manipulate the media and his contacts with government officials to set up causes that he would champion into the future. On January 29, at an informal luncheon for government information officers, Nader stated that there had been no effort by the press or the federal government to make the Freedom of Information Act practical. The law, which had passed on July 4, 1967, requires governmental agencies to release all information to the public, except materials that involve national security. Nader would become more heavily involved in this area as time passed.

JOUSTING WITH NEW ISSUES

March 1968 brought up another issue for Nader when he visited Secretary of the Interior Stewart L. Udall regarding inhumane working conditions in America's coal mines. From this step, Nader would be led into the turmoil of the coal miners' union election the following year. He also attacked the fishing industry, told a Senate subcommittee that GM should be examined under the antitrust laws and broken up and that Rolls Royce should be cited for unsafe door catches. It seemed that Nader had a finger in several consumer-oriented pots.

Nader also became a consulting editor for a new magazine—*Mayday*—a publication started by new-wave muckrakers, such as James Ridgeway, Robert Sherrill, and Andrew Kopkind, in 1968. Nader also took on the fights for safer natural gas pipelines, wholesale poultry products, radiation from medical X rays, and nuclear energy.

Nader's push for safer natural gas pipelines actually began two years earlier, when in a June 29, 1966, speech before the Washington Chapter of the American Society of Safety Engineers, he illustrated the damage caused by a ruptured pipeline in a Natchitoches, Louisiana, housing complex where 17 people died. Many of the more than one-half million miles of lines were too old, badly installed, or even made of wood, which made them dangerous and disasters certain.

In addition to speaking about these dangers to the public, Nader testified before a subcommittee of the Commerce Committee on the dangers of these buried pipelines. Ultimately, a bill was passed by the House on July 26, the Senate on July 31, and signed into law by President Johnson on August 12 as the Natural Gas Pipeline Safety Act of 1968 (PL 90–481). The law required the Transportation secretary to establish acceptable standards for more than 750,000 miles of natural gas pipeline and for gathering lines in residential or commercial areas. Yet again, Nader was disappointed in the strength of the law and the lack of criminal penalties for corporate officers who violated the regulations.

Nader also addressed one of President Johnson's issues from 1967—extending existing federal regulations for meat inspection to the poultry industry. The Wholesome Poultry Products Act was enacted on August 18 and stipulated financial and technical aid to states for developing their own inspection standards, which were required to be at least equal to those of the federal government. This new law affected 1.6 billion pounds of poultry, roughly 13 percent of American consumption.

Once again, however, the rule was not stringent enough for Nader. The law applied only to interstate poultry marketing, as had the original Wholesome Meat Act of 1906. Nader believed that poultry standards needed to be extended to those providing poultry within one state.

Another issue that intrigued and appalled Nader concerned the dangers of X rays and how they were used differently for African Americans than for whites. At a Senate subcommittee hearing, Nader testified that African Americans often received 50 percent stronger doses of X rays because of the assertion that the extra dosage was required for X rays to penetrate darker skin. He also wrote a *New Republic* article entitled "X Ray Exposures" and enlisted the help of reporter Morton Mintz and Congressman E. L. Bartlett from Alaska to present his case to the House of Representatives.

Mintz was successful in digging up a General Electric instruction manual that recommended the higher dosages for African Americans. He was able to corroborate Nader's testimony and assertions and deny the American Dental Association's response to Nader, which claimed Nader was unnecessarily frightening the public.

The result of Nader's and the others' work on this issue was the Radiation Control for Health and Safety Act of October 18, 1968 (Pub. l. 90–602), which included regulation of other products involving radiation, such as microwave ovens, lasers, sun lamps, and televisions. One of the biggest effects related to medical or dental X rays. The primary legislation was not stringent enough to suit Nader; however, over the years, standards have been enormously improved. An article on the Health Physics society Web site reads: "Common practice over the past 30 years may have delivered doses as much as ten times [as those currently given]."[9]

BACK TO THE START WITH A TWIST

After attacking and gaining some ground against these issues, Nader went back to work on the automotive industry, but this time, rather than taking the offensive against an American manufacturer, he set his sites on the German-made Volkswagen. He charged that the Volkswagen was "the most hazardous car currently in use in significant numbers in the United States."[10] He also accused the vehicle of being the most likely to cause fatalities in collisions. He urged that the original Volkswagen Beetle be phased out and that production of the VW microbus stop immediately.

Volkswagen spoke back. Arthur R. Railton, a vice president in the public relations department stated, "We don't have any evidence that the Volkswagen gets into any more accidents than any other car."[11] Still, Nader refused to ride in a Volkswagen and would continue to investigate Volkswagen safety.

To add to the mounting victories with consumer issues in Washington, other consumer legislation was enacted in 1968. A bill authorized the Army Corps of Engineers to begin construction of new water projects in 38 states. The Food and Agriculture Act of 1965 received a permanent extension of regulations covering milk, cotton, wool, feed grains, rice, wheat, and cropland adjustments. Measures were also taken to preserve more of the American wilderness, such as Flaming Gorge National Recreation Area in Utah and Wyoming. Consumerism had taken hold. Nader had become the American people's defender against the wrongs of big business.

With such strong support, he was ready to branch out to even bigger issues. He wanted to evaluate government agencies, congress, and other research-intensive issues. Although Nader worked tirelessly, he would not be able to attack these projects alone. He would need assistance and he knew just where to find it.

NOTES

1. "The Poison Song," *FDA Consumer*, http://vm.cfsan.fda.gov/~lrd/history.html.

2. Upton Sinclair, *The Jungle* (New York: Doubleday, Page, 1906), pp. 112–14.

3. *The Pure Food and Drug Act of 1906*, Public Law 59–384, Sec. 3, 30 June 1906.

4. *The Pure Food and Drug Act of 1906*, Public Law 59–384, Sec. 3, 30 June 1906.

5. Ralph Nader, *The Ralph Nader Reader* (New York: Seven Stories Press, 2000), p. 262.

6. *The Wholesome Meat Act of 1968*, Public Law 90–201, Sec. 17, 15 December 1967.

7. Rosemary Mucklow, USDA Public Forum on Captive Supplies, Denver, CO, 21 September 2000.

8. Quoted in Justin Martin, *Nader, Crusader, Spoiler, Icon* (New York: Perseus, 2002), p. 69.

9. S. Julian Gibbs, DDS, Ph.D., "Radiation from a Lifetime of Dental X rays," *Health Physics Society*, 19 October 2001, http://hps.org/ppublicinformation/ate/q1173.html.

10. Quoted in Ralph de Toledano, *Hit & Run, the Rise—And Fall?—of Ralph Nader* (New Rochelle, NY: Arlington House, 1975), p. 47.

11. Quoted in Charles McCarry, *Citizen Nader* (New York: Saturday Review Press, 1972), p. 117.

Chapter 4

NADER'S RAIDERS

Ralph Nader was not only amassing public support. In 1968, he began to build an army. His causes were just, and young Americans at the time were highly cause-oriented. Many from the boomer[1] generation wanted to be involved in social change. Nader's form of rebellion was more conventional than the radical upheavals forming around the Vietnam War and Civil Rights, and the grape boycott in California had little meaning for them because they couldn't relate to Hispanic migrant farm workers, whose fight had only begun. Nader was part of the so-called old school, trying to change things from within the system, rather than as an SDS Weatherman would,[2] bombing buildings. Nader was just the leader some new Ivy League graduates were looking for.

On January 29, 1968, two friends—Robert C. Fellmeth and Andrew Egendorf, both students at Harvard Law School—were intrigued by what they read about Nader in *Newsweek* and, considering that he had begun looking for assistants, decided to offer their services. They wrote a letter to Nader including the sentence: "Your work is most appealing to two disgusted Harvard graduate students who must endure endless years of drivel in order to mechanically defend the guilty and profitably screw the consumer."[3]

The two young men had no idea how to reach Nader, so they sent their letter to his father in Connecticut, hoping that it would be forwarded because neither Nader's phone number or address were published. Only Nader's special group of reporters had his phone number or address and only one had actually seen his quarters—Ed Mezvinsky, Congressman Neal Smith's legislative assistant, with whom Nader had worked on the

Wholesome Meat Act. Mezvinsky described the room as sparse: No television or any other appliance was evident. He did remember that the footboard of the bed had been removed so that the lanky, six-foot-four Nader could stretch out. This lifestyle fit Nader, considering his crusades. One of Nader's altruist qualities is that he practices what he preaches. Fellmeth and Egendorf admired this quality.

Their letter eventually found its way from Winsted, where they sent it, to Nader. Not long after, Egendorf received a call from Nader around midnight. They discussed the advantages of employing students to help in his work, and Nader mentioned that he had been interested in their letter. He also mentioned that he was interested in gathering a group for a summer project.

Nader had no trouble finding other young people to work with him. By 1968, white middle-class kids had left the Civil Rights movement because young, militant African Americans wanted control of their own group and had shunted the white kids aside. Yet, these cause-oriented orphans were not interested in Timothy Leary's "Turn on, Tune in, Drop out" philosophy. Neither were the disillusioned Eugene McCarthy followers, disappointed by his loss to Richard Nixon in the 1968 presidential election. Nader, on the other hand, was a stalwart figure these idealistic young people could admire and his causes were just. Nader had his choice of well-educated young people willing to give their allegiance to his causes, although the candidates he chose had no background in revolution. Along with Fellmeth and Egendorf came five other eager activists onto Nader's team: Edward Finch Cox, William Howard Taft IV, Judy Areen, Peter Bradford, and John Schultz.

Edward Cox, another student at Princeton, was a senior when Nader tapped him for the team. Cox's family tree also included Robert Livingston, a drafter of the Declaration of Independence. While working for Nader, Cox married President Nixon's daughter Tricia in the Rose Garden at the White House in 1971, and Nader attended the wedding.

William Howard Taft IV also had famous political roots. He was the great-grandson of President William Howard Taft and in his second year at Harvard Law School. He went on to hold many important government posts and became legal advisor to the State Department.

Judy Areen was the daughter of a Chrysler Corporation executive. She had achieved her undergraduate degree at Cornell and was in her third year at Yale Law School. Her selection by Nader shows his total disregard for gender when hiring, although the women's movement in America to gain equality of the sexes had only begun. Areen was not a token woman in the team: Nader only cares about a person's qualifications, and Areen was certainly qualified. She later became the dean of Georgetown Law School.

Peter Bradford seemed to be the only team member without a celebrity pedigree. He graduated from Yale University in 1964 and graduated from Yale Law School the summer the project began. He was a special assistant to the governor of Maine and went on to serve as chair of the New York Public Service Commission and Maine's Public Utilities Commission. He was also commissioner of the U.S. Nuclear Regulatory Commission and currently serves on the board of the Union of Concerned Scientists.

Nader chose John Schultz to lead his team. Schultz was a 29-year-old graduate of Yale Law School and had spent the following years teaching law at the University of Southern California.

Assembled in early June 1968, these seven team members were to be dubbed "Nader's Raiders," and they had a summer of difficult, though interesting, work ahead of them. "As students of Harvard, Yale, and Princeton, we had nothing of the reformer in our backgrounds," they would later write. "[One] had taught for five years at the exclusive Groton School."[4] None of them had experience in navigating the Washington establishment, but they were eager to work hard and eager to learn.

THE PRIMARY INVESTIGATION

An investigation of the Federal Trade Commission (FTC) was their first assignment. Established in 1914, during the Woodrow Wilson administration, the FTC was an independent regulatory agency with the primary responsibility of guaranteeing free and fair competition in American business. The commission was also to protect consumers from poor workmanship and deceptive advertising and bound to publish instances of fraudulent business practices.[5] The president appoints five members of the commission and the chairperson, in concordance with the Senate, to seven-year terms.

In 1938, the FTC's power extended to regulating unfair and deceptive business practices, and the commission was given the power to enforce laws made in accordance with this responsibility. Section 45 of the Federal Trade Commission Act reads, "The Commission is hereby empowered and directed to prevent persons, partnerships, or corporations ... from using unfair methods of competition in or affecting commerce and unfair or deceptive acts or practices in or affecting commerce."[6]

The FTC function is divided into administration and operating bureaus. At the time Nader's Raiders began studying the commission, the bureaus were as follows: deceptive practice, economics, field operation,

industry guidance, restraint of trade, and textiles and furs. The administrative offices were those of secretary, program review officer, general
counsel, hearing examiners, and executive director. The administrative
office handled the general decision-making process of the FTC.

In the opinion of Nader and of his newly formed staff, the FTC was no
longer fulfilling the intentions of the law, and as a young crew, inexperi-
enced in the bureaucracy of the federal government, the Raiders assumed
that the Commission would be forthcoming with information. Unleashed
with zeal and curiosity, they tried to get into every part of the operation,
but were met with evasion and bureaucratic brick walls. They wrote, "Even
simple documents became elusive. One of the first things we needed was a
personnel chart, showing the number of FTC employees and their job clas-
sifications. At first, the Director of Personnel denied that any organization
chart existed."[7] They ran into similar problems when they tried to obtain
budget records; however, when the young lawyers threatened to sue under
the Freedom of Information Act, the records were released to them.

During interviews with some FTC upper-echelon members, the staffers
volunteered only generalized information and with some questions—for
example, a question about the number of lawyers working for the FTC—
the response was that the query would only be answered if placed in writing. One candid source said that the response indicated the general
paranoia in the FTC, which radiated from Chairman Paul Rand Dixon's
office. Eventually, Dixon arranged for a complete lockout of Nader's posse
and prohibited staff members from even speaking with the members of the
investigative team.

This wariness should have been expected. In recent months, Nader
had accused the FTC of siding with the automotive industry concerning
inadequate automobile warranties. Worse, he had embarrassed the Commission in a letter to Washington Senator Warren G. Magnuson, in
which he charged the FTC with slipshod investigation of Volkswagen's
"gray" market reconditioned cars, which were being sold in the United
States as new. Although Nader made it seem as though it were a nation-
wide problem, the FTC maintained that the problem only existed in a
case or two, one being a dealer who had gone out of business before the investigation got underway. Yet, these wounds still stung, and Chairman
Dixon was not about to leave the FTC open to such bombastic charges
from Nader again.

The Raider's inexperience was a fortuitous quality, however, in that the
more they were blocked, the harder they pressed. The law states that it is
any citizen's right to interview a government employee, as long as the em-

ployee agrees to the interview. Their persistence provided interviews with other young FTC lawyers, even if the higher-ups would not cooperate. At the beginning of the team's testimony on their findings, before the Senate Subcommittee on Executive Reorganization, Senator Abraham A. Ribicoff stated, "Bureaucracy being what it is, I am fascinated by your ability to get in so deep, and get so much information."[8]

Before the FTC report was issued in November 1968, the FTC chairman called a hearing at which the Raiders were present. Nader's people felt that this action was scheduled to make them look less credible, and they admit that it almost succeeded. In the impressive setting, with the FTC officials on a dais far above the witnesses, in high-backed chairs and with booming microphones, the young people seemed small. John Schultz acted as the spokesperson for the Nader team, while Dixon kept referring to him as "Mr. Shootz."[9] Andrew Egendorf sat quietly by, taping the hearing. They were not at all daunted. The next day, a reporter from the *Washington Post* gave them their handle, "Nader's Raiders."

The Raiders' report on the FTC was released on January 6, 1969, and was later expanded for the book *Nader's Raiders, Report on the Federal Trade Commission*. Though the entire team provided information for the project, Cox, Fellmeth, and Schultz were its primary authors. They reported that there was ample evidence of indolence and ineptitude in the FTC and cited an incidence of one important official found sleeping in his office with a newspaper over his face. They maintained, however, that their investigation was not exposure of individual employees but, rather, a description of how the FTC was not fulfilling its missions.

Once the report was released, some pointed out that it abounded with quotations that could not be attributed to specific employees and that its assertions were not supported by fact. When Dixon read the report, he was outraged and said that the Raiders picked only on the FTC's faults but listed none of its accomplishments. Still, the report included many efficient suggestions for change that many within the FTC agreed were reasonable.

In the wake of the Raiders' report, a separate and independent investigation of the FTC was carried out by the American Bar Association (ABA). In its report of September 17, 1969, the ABA cited ineffective and divided leadership, incompetence, misallocation of funds, and failure to establish goals and set priorities. Many of these charges were similar to the report levied by Nader's team, as were their recommendations. In turn, President Nixon replaced Dixon with Caspar W. Weinberger, who implemented sweeping changes throughout the commission and caused many important actions to take effect within a short period. It was a victory for the Raiders, and therefore, a victory for Nader.

PROMOTING A MARTYR

Nader was involved in many projects at once, and another with serious implications cropped up that summer—he championed a cause that became mired in corruption, scandal, and ultimately murder. On the night of May 3, 1969, Nader met with three other men at the offices of a Washington, D.C., law firm. The meeting was like something out of a James Bond novel—each approached the meeting from different directions in total secrecy. The men were Joseph A. ("Jock") Yablonski, his brother Leon Yablonski, and Leon's son Steven, all with important ties to the United Mine Workers of America (UMWA). They all had worked in the mines, risen in the ranks of the union, and had now made the decision to discuss the sordid operations of the union with an outsider—Ralph Nader.

Nader had shown himself to be a campaigner for the mineworkers' plight in the newspapers and on television. He told people how 1 in 2 people who worked in the mines suffered from black lung disease[10] and that 1 in 30 miners was injured each year. He had denounced the UMWA for its dispassionate attitude about the suffering of miners.

The UMWA had fallen under the leadership of W. A. (Tony) Boyle, who had succeeded labor leader John L. Lewis, president of the UMWA from 1920 to 1960. Boyle was up for reelection that year. According to the web site Appalachian Power, "It was an ordinary sight for miners to display on the walls in their homes the picture of John L. Lewis right beside the Saints."[11] Boyle was Lewis's boy, so there was no doubt that Boyle would continue with another five-year term. Boyle often controlled the rank and file with violent men. No candidate dared to challenge him.

Jock Yablonski was the former president of the Pittsburgh chapter of the UMWA (District 5); acting director of the Non-Partisan league, the political branch of the UMWA; a member of the international executive board; and a 35-year UMWA member. He was appalled by Boyle's tactics and opposed him in several instances, including over the 1965 passage of a law to extend benefits for black lung survivors. Boyle had been against the increase of an additional $75 to mine workers who suffered from occupational diseases; he saw it as too costly. Yablonski disagreed and influenced a few Pennsylvania state senators and Governor William Scranton to back the bill. Boyle saw Yablonski's tactics as insubordinate and forced him to resign as president of District 5.

Then, the Consolidated Coal number nine mine in Farmington, West Virginia, exploded on November 20, 1968. Boyle showed up at the mine, dressed in a suit with a rose in his lapel, and praised Consolidated Coal's safety record. Yet, of the 99 miners working, 78 had to be left inside because there was no way to stop the continuing explosions and fires. The mine had to be closed off. As another insult to the rank and file, Boyle also refused to speak to the victims' families.

Yablonski compared Boyle's behavior with that of Lewis, who had donned a hard hat and gone into the West Frankfort, Illinois, mine after it exploded on December 21, 1951, and emerged with a sooty face and a heavy heart. His anguish was captured in a photograph for all miners to see. "That picture just had to make coal miners feel so proud," Yablonski told his son. "But that sonovabitch Boyle. With those people dead in the mine, how could that bastard stand up and praise the company's safety record the way he did?"[12] Soon after the Farmington disaster, Nader became involved.

Even after such bubbling animosity, Yablonski had no plans to run against Boyle in an expensive, tiring, and potentially dangerous election when he met Nader, although Yablonski had toyed with the idea earlier. His family and friends had discouraged him. Nader came right out and asked if Yablonski would run and said that he would support Yablonski in the election. Yablonski looked at Nader and said, "If I do run, Ralph, they'll try to kill me."[13] Nader replied, "They wouldn't dare—you'll be in a goldfish bowl."[14]

During the next three weeks, Yablonski and Nader met to discuss the union, usually beginning around midnight and ending around five in the morning. Secrecy was important while Yablonski weighed his options. He told Nader that if he made the decision to run, he would need the support of Congressman Ken Hechler of West Virginia, three prominent doctors who had educated miners about and fought against black lung disease in West Virginia, and Nader himself. Yablonski did not make up his mind to run until just before he made his announcement.

AGAINST THE MACHINE

Yablonski's objectives were to purify the union, to return to a democratic process, and to protect the health and safety of its members. "Union democracy," said Yablonski, "is the single most important issue in the campaign for election of a new United Mine Workers of America (UMW) president."[15] Just after his ascendancy to president, Boyle had concentrated his power by making union districts trusteeships, which meant that district leaders could no longer be elected, but only appointed by Boyle himself. He had also raised the support of pensioners by increasing their monthly benefit. Boyle's practices only set miner against miner—those for Boyle and, like Yablonski, those against Boyle.

For his part, Nader had put Gary Sellers to work in Washington, watching the Coal Mine Health and Safety bill. In West Virginia, Davitt McAteer (current head of the Mine Safety and Health Administration), a law student who had created his own team of young lions to help in the fight, took his recruits to Washington to be part of Nader's team, already investigating mine safety in West Virginia. For the cause, McAteer had raised $9,280 including a donation from Nader himself.

Jock's son Joseph A. "Chip" Yablonski resigned his job as an attorney for the National Labor Relations Board to become Jock's campaign manager. Nader assigned Sellers to be his representative with the Yablonskis throughout the election and discussed his methods of using the press and how to sway miners' loyalties toward Jock Yablonski by disclosing the violence occurring in the union with the candidate and his staff. Nader urged Yablonski to reawaken the miners' feelings for Lewis and their miner's pride. Yablonski saw Nader as a dynamic leader and followed Nader's advice, but Yablonski was destined to lose the election by the action of Boyle's men, who tampered with the votes. Yablonski's fate was sealed even before he announced his candidacy on May 29, 1969.

Winning the election did not satisfy Tony Boyle. Jock Yablonski knew that the election had been tainted and clamored for an investigation. Because Yablonski was so vocal and would not tolerate Boyle's actions, the anticipated horror struck in the early days of January 1970. Yablonski was murdered, along with his wife and daughter, in a contract killing ordered by Boyle. The killers were caught and sentenced soon after, but Boyle remained free another five years, until he was arrested and charged. He was convicted of conspiracy to commit murder and given a life sentence. He died in jail in 1985.

The Coal Mine Health and Safety Act of 1969 was the positive element in this tragedy because it protected American miners from the abuses that had gone for more than a century. Although he lost his life, Yablonski remains in the hearts of many miners. Paul Lemmon, a union official said, "Jock was a great man. If it wasn't for him, I wouldn't be sitting in this seat today. Because of his democratic movement, anyone can run for office in the union without interference. At one time the mine workers were dominated from the top."[16]

THE FIRST BRICK IN A SOLID ORGANIZATION

Along with the UMWA election, Nader's Raiders found the summer of 1969 a busy time. Nader decided his operation needed a hub and so, through several foundation grants and the money he had earned on *Unsafe at Any Speed*, he founded the Center for the Study of Responsive Law. A building was even leased for the operation, and during 1969 and part of 1970, it held offices on Dupont Circle in Washington, D.C. The place was a crumbling brick mansion, complete with turrets and gables. Across the street, derelicts congregated with their brown paper bags holding cheap liquor or wine. Dupont Circle was also the center of the D.C. hippie movement. The Raiders were clearly not part of that scene, with their short haircuts and suits. Occasionally, they lost a typewriter because an indigent came through the unlocked doors of the Center and stole one.

Inside was a buzzing hive of activity. Nader hired 200 Raiders from among the 30,000 applications received that summer for the plum positions. One attraction was that the staff had complete freedom to attack the targets Nader set for them, such as the Food and Drug Administration's lack of attention to the food industry, mine safety, the hazards of air pollution, and the Department of Agriculture. However, the salary was well below par. He paid each Raider between $150 and $300 a week for the entire summer, providing they could not meet the expenses themselves. The attitude was "anything for the good of the projects"—late working hours, even on Sundays and holidays, no vacations, no Cokes, total dedication. The Raiders were expected to be motivated to change society for the better before they ever reached Washington, D.C. One former Raider, Sheila Harty, wrote, "As a Nader Raider, I was an avenging angel against modern sins, like environmental pollution, occupational disease and injury, deceptive advertising, and corporate accountability. In fact, I've never since been so content with employment. I often wondered why I felt so at home."[17]

Yet, some Raiders questioned Nader's uninvolvement in the issues of the Vietnam War and Civil Rights. One even spoke of this neglect as avoidance; Nader later met with the young man and the remark was retracted. "What is more intimately involved with civil rights and poverty than the invisible violence of the corporations? Who do they think gets cheated, diseased, crippled, and generally screwed if not the minorities and the poor?"[18]

That summer, Fellmeth returned from the Raiders' successful review of the FTC to concentrate on a new project—the Interstate Commerce Commission (ICC), a commission set up by Congress in 1887 to represent and protect the public interest in the transportation of interstate commerce, originally applying to the railroads but subsequently involving trucking, as well. Leading a team of six young lawyers, Fellmeth and other Raiders produced the report, *The Interstate Commerce Omission, The Public Interest and the ICC*. The first inflammatory sentence of the book came from Nader's forward: "As the oldest independent federal regulatory agency, the Interstate Commerce Commission has set longevity records in its systematic failure to protect or further the public interest in surface transportation."[19] The investigative team found that the commission appointments had been made based on politics alone, making it "unqualified and weak."[20] Some of the committee's other findings were as follows:

> The ICC is now primarily a forum at which private transportation interests settle their disputes.
>
> As a passive forum, the ICC has failed to provide for any useful mechanism for the representation of the public interest in the development of the record.
>
> The Commission's upper staff has a collective personality of extreme conservatism, with all policy recommendations made from within the framework of conditions extant in the 1930s.
>
> Further precluding the possibility of a public interest perspective is the Commission's relationship with industry—which can be generously described as "intimate."
>
> The ICC has numerous advisory groups to help set policy at the initial, formative stages within the agency—including not one consumer or consumer representative.
>
> Job interchange levels between the ICC and industry have grown, with "deferred bribes" becoming the norm.
>
> Congressional oversight has not affected agency policy.
>
> Relations between the ICC and the public have been nonexistent.[21]

The final heavy blow from the committee reads, "There is evidence of deep corruption at the ICC, beyond 'politics' and favoritism."[22]

FALLING OUT OF FAVOR

These were strong charges, but the Raiders were analyzing the workings of more than one agency. James S. Turner led another group of Raiders against the Food and Drug Administration and produced the report, *The Chemical Feast*. Another major investigation led to national headlines but bad press for the Nader group: *Vanishing Air*, a report on air pollution by John C. Esposito and Larry J. Silverman.

As with all reports Nader sponsored, he authored the forward to the book, and it began with an inflammatory sentence: "The pervasive environmental violence of air pollutants has imperiled health, safety, and property throughout the nation for many decades."[23] That statement did not cause Nader to lose face with Congress, but another statement most certainly did: "Although this book brings to light many hitherto undisclosed facts and events, its most significant contribution is its analysis of the collapse of the federal air pollution effort starting with Senator Edmund Muskie and continuing to the pathetic abatement efforts and auto pollution policies of NAPCA [National Air Pollution Control Administration]."[24]

Senator Edmund Muskie of Maine, who was in charge of the Subcommittee on Air and Water Pollution, found the report to be a personal attack, as did the reporters in his camp. Muskie had run for president in the 1968 election, and many people liked and trusted him on Capitol Hill. He was the frontrunner for the Democratic presidential candidate in 1972, and people who supported him did not approve of a Nader-sponsored project in which Muskie was degraded.

A promoter of the Air Quality Act of 1967, Muskie's record on environmental pollutants was widely admired. The bill required a 90 percent reduction in pollution from automobile exhaust by 1975 and included a $465 million budget for research. However, *Vanishing Air* states that there was obviously something nefarious about the law: "[When the legislation was passed] American industry... breathed a collective sigh of relief. Everyone seemed to be pleased with the new law—in this case, a sure sign that something was wrong."[25]

The report goes on to accuse Muskie of compromising the bill to suit the White House, Congress, and industry, saying that Muskie had made the bill more complex, less threatening, and a law that industry could support, a bill less concerned with its impact on consumers than on industry's bottom line. And Muskie's temperament was challenged: "It is hard to avoid the belief that Muskie, an extremely astute politician who by temperament avoids conflict and unfavorable odds, was influenced by a desire to get the bill through Congress with a minimum of acrimony. He therefore took the path of least resistance."[26] The report even invited Muskie to resign from the subcommittee.

Muskie, hoping to take his record on air pollution into the 1972 presidential election, quickly rebutted the Nader team's report with a public statement, saying that he had done his best and that he was in no way involved with the dark conspiracy the report had put forth. Nader and Esposito maintained that they had made an honorable attack on Muskie's record alone, not a personal evaluation.

Through all of this, the book became less the straightforward report it was intended to be, and more a national tempest. Muskie supporters were outraged and began to view Nader and his cohorts as antagonists. Muskie's staff rebutted *Vanishing Air* in an 85-page report. Nader remained aloof and continued to support Esposito and the validity of his work, though later he admitted that the report may have gone too far.

HINTS OF ALIENATION

Nader continued to gather negative press when he attacked Senator A. Ribicoff on a bill to create a consumer protection agency, which had been one of Nader's primary interests for years. He thought that an entity to answer consumer complaints, to educate consumers, and to conduct product research was vital to making corporations responsible. Nader wanted the new agency to be independent, such as the FTC, answerable to consumers alone. Many of his hours were put into this project, which often took precedence over other causes.

On December 1, 1970, a bill to create such an agency came to a vote on the Senate floor. Nader and Sellers, who had worked so diligently with the UMWA election, were in the gallery. Unhappy with the way things were going, the two continually sent messages to the senators and their assistants. Nader found the bill weakening before his eyes, and before long, he sent a message into the contingent of reporters there, saying the bill had become the worst piece of legislation he had ever seen, and placed the blame for the watering down on its floor manager—Nader's former ally, Ribicoff. Nader accused Ribicoff of "intolerable erosions"[27] in the bill.

Both Nader and Sellers had tried to provide potentially strengthening amendments for Ribicoff's Subcommittee on Executive Reorganization, to no avail. However, Senator Philip Hart of Michigan told Nader that he would introduce amendments to the floor that would allow both sides— one that wanted little presidential involvement and the other that wanted full participation—satisfaction. The plan was to allow the president, the speaker of the House, and the Senate majority leader each to appoint three members to the agency's board, among other strengthening provisions. However, Ribicoff felt that his committee's version of the bill should have been satisfactory to Nader, and he refused to accept any amendments on the floor. Nader felt that Ribicoff had betrayed him and was not fazed when he saw the weak bill killed in the House Rules Committee.

Once again, reporters felt that Nader's attack on a U.S. senator, this time Ribicoff, was harsh. Even after the law was finally passed that created the Consumer Protection Agency on October 14, 1971, Nader complained that the law had been stripped of its "integrity and effectiveness."[28] Ribicoff was quite disenchanted by Nader's remarks and felt that he had worked toward the creation of a worthwhile agency, but that Nader could not be satisfied unless the legislation was completely up to Nader's standard. Common knowledge has it that Congress runs on compromise. Rarely is a bill introduced that need not be changed in some way or another to suit everyone in question. Ribicoff felt that he had provided the best legislation he could, which was better than no legislation at all. His attitude about Nader's petulance had also begun to permeate the Senate.

Another of Nader's causes in 1969 was to get the Federal Aviation Administration (FAA) to ban smoking on all flights, and on December 9, Nader heavily criticized the railroads for dumping, according to his estimate, "two hundred million pounds of human excrement"[29] on railroad tracks each year. He also made a speech at Miss Porter's School in Farmington, Connecticut, an exclusive all-girls prep school, where he would find a new type of Raider, Raiders he sent on another meaningful quest.

NOTES

1. Those born between 1946 and 1964.

2. Some members of the Students for a Democratic Society (SDS) branched off to form the Weathermen in the late 1960s. Their aim was to overthrow the United States government through any means possible. They were responsible for several bombings around the country in the early 1970s.

3. Quoted in Justin Martin, *Nader, Crusader, Spoiler, Icon* (New York: Perseus, 2002), p. 75.

4. Edward F. Cox, Robert C. Fellmeth, and John E. Schulz, *Nader's Raiders, Report on the Federal Trade Commission* (New York: Richard W. Baron, 1969; reprint, New York: Grove Press, 1970), p. 3 (reprint ed.).

5. The FTC mandate does not include banks and common carriers (companies that transport goods or messages to the public for a fee, such as trucking companies or telecommunications firms), which are supervised by other agencies.

6. Federal Trade Commission Act, 15 U.S.C., §§ 41–51, Section 45, paragraph 2.

7. Cox, Fellmeth, and Schulz, *Nader's Raiders, Report on the Federal Trade Commission*, p. 6.

8. Cox, Fellmeth, and Schulz, *Nader's Raiders, Report on the Federal Trade Commission*, p. 9.

9. Quoted in Charles McCarry, *Citizen Nader* (New York: Saturday Review Press, 1972), p. 189.

10. Coal workers' pneumoconiosis or black lung disease is caused by the inhalation of coal dust.

11. "Yablonski Murder," *Appalachian Power*, http://www.appalachianpower. com/yablonski%20murder.htm.

12. Trevor Armbrister, *Act of Vengeance: The Yablonski Murders and Their Solution*. (New York: Saturday Review Press, 1975), p. 39.

13. Quoted in McCarry, *Citizen Nader*, p. 241.

14. Quoted in McCarry, *Citizen Nader*, p. 241.

15. "What Is Union Democracy?" *The Association for Union Democracy*, 2000, http://www.uniondemocracy.com/Home/whatitis.htm.

16. Quoted in Joe Barsotti, "Ex-For Examining the Yablonski in Book," *Pittsburgh Press*, 10 June 1990, p. W1.

17. Sheila Harty, "Ethics of Citizenship from a Nader Raider," 1998, http://www.the-sandcastle.com/sheila/Ethics%20of%20Citizenship%20from% 20a%20Nader%20Raider.doc.

18. Quoted in McCarry, *Citizen Nader*, p. 199.

19. Robert C. Fellmeth, *The Interstate Commerce Omission, The Public Interest and the ICC* (New York: Grossman, 1970), p. vii.

20. Fellmeth, *The Interstate Commerce Omission, The Public Interest and the ICC*, p. 311.

21. Fellmeth, *The Interstate Commerce Omission, The Public Interest and the ICC*, pp. 311–13.

22. Fellmeth, *The Interstate Commerce Omission, The Public Interest and the ICC*, p. 313.

23. John C. Esposito and Larry J. Silverman, *Vanishing Air*, Forward by Ralph Nader, (New York: Grossman, 1970), p. vii.

24. Esposito and Silverman, *Vanishing Air*, p. viii.

25. Esposito and Silverman, *Vanishing Air*, p. 270.

26. Esposito and Silverman, *Vanishing Air*, p. 273.

27. Quoted in Martin, *Nader, Crusader, Spoiler, Icon*, p. 117.

28. Quoted in McCarry, *Citizen Nader*, p. 236.

29. Quoted in McCarry, *Citizen Nader*, p. 117.

Chapter 5

THE GOLDEN YEARS

The year 1970 was intense and volatile. In February, the Chicago Seven were acquitted of conspiracy to incite riots at the 1968 Democratic National Convention; however, five were found guilty of crossing state lines with intent to incite rioting and with delivery of inflammatory speeches to aid in the process. The defendants called themselves Yippies, members of the Youth International Party, and they vehemently protested the war in Vietnam. In response to their convictions, further demonstrations broke out across the country, and many arrests ensued when demonstrators became confrontational and even violent with police.

Most assuredly, the war was at the forefront of dissention in 1970. Feelings ran high on both sides of the issue when it was disclosed in March that a company of Army men massacred an entire village of Vietnamese neutrals at Mai Lai. People who had been staunch supporters of the war began to question the effect of the war on the men fighting it. Even primarily peaceful demonstrations turned violent in May, when students threw rocks at National Guardsmen at Kent State University in Kent, Ohio, and four students were shot by young soldiers who feared for their lives. Two black students were also shot by police at Jackson State in Mississippi under similar circumstances. The public began to see that the war had not only taken young men into battle, but that America's sons and daughters were also being shot on their own streets.

Yet, 1970 did have its positive events. On April 1, President Richard Nixon signed Public Law 91–222 (the Public Health Cigarette Smoking Act) to ban cigarette advertising on radio and television.[1] In April, Apollo XIII astronauts James A. Lovell, John L. Swigert, and Fred W.

Haise Jr. made it home after a spacecraft malfunction nearly cost them their lives. The topic of women's rights was coming to the forefront as the Women's Strike for Equality was held in August, led by Betty Friedan, Gloria Steinem, and Ivy Bottini, carrying an enormous banner that screamed "WOMEN OF THE WORLD UNITE!"

Big changes were coming for the country, though the enormous impact of these would not be recognized for some time. In 1970, it was impossible for people to hide in their homes and not know what was going on around them. Horrible images from the war in Vietnam were blasted into American living rooms each night on the evening news—on television, which had only been widely available within the past decade. Viewers saw police beating demonstrators in the streets, militant Civil Rights marchers threatening to kill those who stood in the way of their freedom, and Charles Manson's crew be convicted of a senseless blood bath, which took the lives of several innocent victims, including that of actress Sharon Tate and her unborn child. The peace and complacency Americans had basked in after the Allied victory in World War II had begun to unravel with the assassination of President John F. Kennedy in 1963 and the subsequent live television broadcast of the murder of his accused assassin, Lee Harvey Oswald. In this unsettling time, the issues and events were not merely words on a page or voices on a radio; they were broadcast images of the messy state of our union.

No matter the ugliness or the glamour of our daily news, Ralph Nader's main thrust was and continues to be that each of us bears the duty of responsible citizenship. To be able to carry out these duties, each citizen must be well versed in current events. Only through this thorough understanding is it possible to confront the ills in our system of government. Nader continued to read six newspapers each day and refused to even speak when riding in a car for a long time, as he religiously continued to search the newspapers, always eager to spot an ill that needed a remedy.

By 1970, Nader had become increasingly disenchanted with Congress. The legislation he was able to take part in developing became unrecognizable before the bill was passed in several instances. In others, there were no criminal penalties for executives who broke the law. He lost faith in using Congress for legislation that was adequate. So, he turned to grassroots or local-level politics in his quest for consumer protection.

NADER AND THE MAIDEN MUCKRAKERS

On November 20, 1969, Nader traveled to Miss Porter's School in Farmington, Connecticut, where he spoke before an audience of young women. This independent boarding school was founded in 1843 for girls in grades 9 through 12 and in 1970 was still a finishing school, with the prime intention of shaping young women into model homemakers. Mainly for girls from affluent families, this boarding school boasts "ancients" (alumna) such as former First Lady Jacqueline Kennedy Onasis and etiquette expert Leticia Baldridge. When Nader spoke to Miss Porter's students, among the crowd were young women with high-profile parents, including Claire Townsend, the daughter of Avis CEO Robert Townsend, with whom Nader had become acquainted.

Nader's message of getting out and changing the world was highly successful. Lallie Lloyd, another member of the audience for that speech, said, "He's a very passionate speaker and was very charismatic. Nader's visionary sense of justice was very appealing to me, as was his basic sense of fairness. His attitude and expectation that government should be helping people, especially vulnerable people, was quite inspiring."[2] As the speech ended, several of the young women from the 230-person audience came to speak to Nader and ask him questions. They wanted to know how they could join the fight, and soon Nader realized a new, enthusiastic team of investigative workers could be formed from sedate Miss Porter's School.

Nursing homes would be their target, and six recent graduates from Miss Porter's volunteered to form the new group: Claire Townsend, Lallie Lloyd, Janet Keyes, Catherine Morgan, Patricia Pitiff, and Elizabeth "Liz" Baldwin. The young women spent the summer in Washington, D.C., with their 25-year-old teacher, Margaret Quinn, as their chaperone. Lloyd said, "Claire was also a very charismatic person. She was one of the student leaders on campus and so, when she stepped forward and said, 'Hey, does anybody want to work with me on this?,' it was an easy question to respond to. At the same time, it didn't come without a cost. Most of us were used to doing fun things with our families over the summer. [With this project] I would be working alone in Washington. So, that was a first step for me. It was the first time I had to literally work all summer long and we knew that going into it. It wasn't just like this was a sort of fly-by-night response. It required some commitment."[3]

When the press learned of this new venture, they dubbed the young women Maiden Muckrakers. Lloyd said, "I feel in terms of the assignment that I was given, I was in way over my head. My father, at the time, was an investment banker, so I was given the SEC, as if at the age of seventeen I could really understand it, and I was supposed to be investigating the economic structures of the nursing home industry and the whole question about how they were regulated as economic entities. Clearly, just raising the whole question of, 'Should people be making a profit taking care of frail or elderly people?' "[4]

Yet, each of them played a vital role in the process. Nader said, "They worked in nursing homes, they came to Washington, they researched, they wrote a book [*Old Age: The Last Segregation*], and then they went on radio and TV, testified before Congress. And all this concern led to one of our associates starting the National Coalition for Nursing Home Reform, and she's still at it, with chapters all over the country."[5]

This was true of any Raider who became involved with a special project. Although they earned little money, what they gained in experience and exposure was well worth the effort, though they seemed more interested in changing the world than in making names for themselves. Claire Townsend, who died in 1995 of breast cancer, went on to work in the film industry and was a vice president at United Artists and Twentieth Century Fox. Lallie Lloyd has become an independent consultant and worked with such esteemed institutions as the Rockefeller Foundation and the Pew Charitable Trusts.

Other Raiders of note are Robert C. Fellmeth, who is the executive director of Children's Advocacy Institute and law professor at the University of San Diego School of Law. Andrew Egendorf is president and CEO of Tradecraft Corporation, an intellectual property holding company based in the Boston area. Another of Nader's acolytes is Byron Bloch, who became a renowned consumer activist. "Ralph was the key catalyst in launching my work in auto safety," Bloch stated.[6] In only one remarkable trip to Washington, D.C., Bloch pointed out to Nader that the big auto manufacturers were charging $23–$25 for safety belts in passenger automobiles, when they cost the manufacturer only $3.50–$4.00 each, whether for luxury or economy cars. "Ralph typed a press release on his portable typewriter and sent it to Ribicoff, who immediately called a hearing," Bloch said. "The end result was a savings of $16 million a year for consumers."[7] Today, Bloch continues his friendship with Nader and the fight for auto and traffic safety through myriad interviews on such prestigious shows as *60 Minutes*, *Nightline* and *20/20*. In 2001, he won a lifetime achievement award at the 12th Annual World Traffic Safety Symposium. Other Nadarites have gone on to become writers or prominent attorneys, and many have stayed with Nader to continue their consumer protection work.

CAMPAIGN GM

One cause that never left Nader was the dream of toppling General Motors (GM). In 1970, he was approached by another pair of Harvard law graduates, Geoffrey Cowan and Philip Moore, who had a plan. They had been mired in an attempt to get Harvard to divest itself of holdings in

Mississippi Power and Light Company and had tried to pressure shareholders of Dow Chemical to get the company to stop manufacturing napalm, an incendiary jelly of polystyrene, benzene, and gasoline used in bomb making. Napalm was used extensively by the United States during the Vietnam War. Both of Cowan and Moore's fights had been fruitless, but they had a new and quite interesting plan.

If they could convince major shareholders of large corporations to sell their holdings because they were unhappy with the corporation's practices, they could create a financial crisis for the corporation because whenever large blocks of stock are sold, the value of shares will naturally decline. Cowan and Moore also planned to organize a group of people unhappy with the corporation and charge them with buying one share of stock, thus giving them the right to attend the annual meeting, to vote, and to speak. In this way, group members could make their concerns known. If the corporation was unreceptive to their wishes and if the group was large enough, group members could sell off their single shares of stock, which would also create instability in the corporation's worth. This action should cause the corporation's management and board of directors to seriously consider changing policies connected with the sell-off.

When Nader met Cowan and Moore, they had come up with a plan to attack General Motors, Nader's nemesis, and they had raised $40,000 to fund the endeavor. Cowan and Moore planned to attend the GM annual meeting on May 22, 1970, where they intended to make demands of the corporation. Their goals were to insist that GM manufacture cars that were less polluting, make factories safer for employees, and recall defective products more quickly. Cowan and Moore also wanted to propose increasing the members on GM's board of directors by three: Ralph Nader, economist John Kenneth Galbraith, and John Gardner, founder of Common Cause, a campaign finance reform organization.

Nader's lawsuit for invasion of privacy was still in process, so Nader felt it would be a conflict of interest for him to serve on GM's board, even if he could get elected; however, he was enthusiastic about their plan and agreed to help with media attention and strategy. Thus began the Project on Corporate Responsibility—in short, Campaign GM.

To launch the campaign, Nader organized a press conference at the Mayflower Hotel in Washington, D.C., which was held on February 7, 1970. He told the news corps, "The basic thrust of the campaign will be to alert and inform the public about their omnipresent neighbor, General Motors, and how it behaves."[8] Nader also remarked that though he was behind the campaign, he would not be directly involved. With this, GM was put on alert—the annual meeting would be very different from those of years gone by. Campaign GM members intended to point out their issues to GM's nearly 1.5 million shareholders, hoping to force GM to decrease its 35 percent share of the country's water and air pollution and to increase auto safety standards for their vehicles.

To achieve these goals, Cowan and Moore first came up with a list of nine resolutions, including a motion to increase minority hiring in management positions and a call for GM to lobby for improvements in mass transit, disregarding the corporation's history for being anti–mass transit. The resolutions were submitted to GM management in letters on February 6 and 22, asking that these be included in the company's proxy statement, which is sent to each investor. The proxy statement includes a ballot so that shareholders may vote on proposed resolutions, even if they are not able to attend an annual meeting. As expected, however, GM flatly refused to include the resolutions in the proxy statement.

In response to GM's refusal, Campaign GM filed a complaint with the Securities and Exchange Commission (SEC), and on March 19, the SEC discarded seven of Campaign GM's nine resolutions but did order that two be included in the proxy statement, thus allowing the issues to be decided by shareholder vote. One of the resolutions upheld by the SEC was for GM to include consumer-friendly members on its board of directors. As with Nader, Galbraith and Gardner declined to run and a new slate of three candidates was formed: former consumer advisor to President Lyndon B. Johnson, Betty Furness; Pulitzer Prize–winning biologist René Dubois; and prominent Civil Rights leader, now a spokesperson for the United States Attorney's Office, Channing Phillips.

GROUNDBREAKING RESULTS

The other proposal approved by the SEC established a shareholders' committee, which would include people from all occupations and lifestyles. The committee would have full access to all GM records and monitor GM's consumer-related and business performance. The SEC, however, had to be sure that the proxy issues were worded so that GM would still be run by its board. Former SEC Commissioner Richard B. Smith stated, "We did a lot of fussing with the shareholder proposal rules for proxy statements...attempting to refine it in a way that gave an appropriate vent to shareholder voices, but without compromising the basic responsibility of the board of directors, once it was elected, to manage the affairs of the company."[9] Once the final resolutions were designed, GM had no choice but to comply with the SEC's order.

Campaign GM's interaction with the SEC was groundbreaking. Never before had a group of citizens used these tactics to cause a big corporation to accede to their wishes. Today, the committee's actions are noted as the historic turning point whereby corporations became more answerable to its shareholders and to consumers for its policies and actions. Carrying the action even further, Mayor John V. Lindsay of New York asked the city worker's pension board to use their voting rights of 162,000 shares to "urge development of pollution-free cars and to help improve mass transit transportation."[10]

The fact that the proposals were defeated did not decrease the impact of Campaign GM's actions. In addition to the step taken by Lindsay, Amherst College and Brown, Yale, and Stanford Universities, among others, used their voting shares to back the resolution for adding three additional members to the GM board of directors. Though the corporation was under no obligation to do so, GM still stepped up and created a Public Policy Committee on August 31. Campaign GM's message had gotten through, and one of the corporate mega-giants had bowed to the will of the people. This victory helped keep the consumerism fires burning.

Always interested in getting young people excited about civics and activism, Nader also went back to Winsted in 1970 to deliver the Gilbert School commencement address. He told students, "Almost every significant breakthrough has come from the spark, the drive, the initiative of one person. You must believe this."[11] This concept was given to Nader by his father, who said, "The greatest obstacle to good government in a democracy is the feeling by too many citizens that they just don't count."[12]

Nader has spent his entire life trying to make people understand that they can make a difference. And he's done it via example, rather than words. Nader eats only natural foods, as he was trained to do by his mother. Even today, he lives a frugal lifestyle and funnels the money he earns back into his consumer-citizen "machine." He also refuses to ride in a Volkswagen, which he considered the most dangerous car on the road. Lallie Lloyd of the Maiden Muckraker group told an anecdote about this: "During the summer, when a meeting we had attended was over, we were walking out into the parking lot to get into Claire's car and we offered [Nader] a ride. We were going to drop him off wherever he wanted to be dropped off. But when we got to the car, he wouldn't go with us. As it turned out, she was driving a Volkswagen, and he wouldn't ride in Volkswagens!"[13]

FOR THE PEOPLE

Nader is a staunch believer in each of his causes, and in the 1970s, he continued to testify before various congressional committees on mine safety, mercury pollution, unfair credit practices, and railroad dumping, and he lobbied for three months for the establishment of a consumer protection agency, to no avail. In 1970, he also moved the Center for the Study of Responsive Law because the Victorian building they occupied was to be torn down and replaced with a Metropolitan Transit (Metro) station. Their new offices would be just a few blocks away, in a more modern building with carpeting and air-conditioning, where Nader would have an office of his own, with a hand-painted "1" on his door. He would not run the center, however. For that position, he hired an old friend from Harvard, Ted Jacobs. The rent was $1,200 a month, and for that and many other expenses, the Center needed funding.

Nader settled his lawsuit against General Motors on August 13 and received $425,000, which was the highest amount collected in an invasion of privacy case to that time. One news report stated, "GM said the settlement was not an admission of guilt by the company and was merely an effort to avoid further expenses and personnel time."[14] Nader vowed to use the funds to continue his watch of GM practices in consumer-related areas.

After legal expenses, Nader realized $280,000 (comparable to $2,050,000 in 2003 when measured against the gross domestic product [GDP] per capita).[15] He invested the money in a new legal firm and labeled it the Public Interest Research Group (PIRG). The law practice was dedicated to representing the public in suits against corporations, and he wanted it to be as powerful and influential as the Washington firm of Covington & Burling, another of Nader's nemeses and a mirror organization for what he intended for his PIRG.

Led by Dean Atcheson, former Secretary of State in the Truman administration, the 50-plus-year-old Covington & Burling represented about two-fifths of the nation's five hundred most important corporations in 1970 and employed only the top lawyers in the country, most of them Ivy League. Nader quickly hired 13 young attorneys at a salary of $4,500 per year, which would be equivalent to $18,300 in 2003,[16] to staff his PIRG, and though the income, the prestigious office, and all other perks connected to a firm such as Covington & Burling were missing, these young banner-carrying predators were eager to fight for the public against the big corporate machine.

To head his project, he drafted 32-year-old Gary Sellers, who had worked on the mine safety issues and the UMWA elections. Sellers had also worked for Covington & Burling, in budget administration, during the Johnson administration and had headed a study for Nader on workplace safety, which aided in the passage of the Occupational Health and Safety Act (OSHA) of 1970.

The PIRG set up offices on 15th Street NW, and lacking furniture at the outset, Nader addressed his group while they sat on the floor. He instructed his new team to read—everything and anything because that was the only way to be versed on the day-to-day workings of the world. He also set assignments for the young lawyers, which included studies on the environment, tax policies, health care, and banking. He wanted them to attack cases within their realms, but only those cases that directly affected the public. Before long, the PIRG was inundated with cases. Two of the first had to do with petitioning the FDA to include stronger warnings on birth control pills and alerting the FTC to false advertising claims by Bristol Meyers regarding Excedrin, which claimed to have twice the effectiveness of aspirin.

Unleashing his hungry and quick hunting dogs, Nader waited for results and went on to expand his idea. Independently, the attorneys would have to investigate their assignment, and produce a monthly progress report. Each attorney had to prepare his or her own reports because there were no secretaries. In fact, all correspondence was handled by the attorneys, and Nader encouraged the diligent use of mimeographing, rather than photocopying, which at the time was much more expensive. The services were always at the expense of the PIRG itself. Nader measured the firm's success by how much money they had saved the public not by how many hours were billed to others.

DEVELOPING A NETWORK

Early in the development of the first PIRG, Nader realized how viable a vehicle it was for action. Quite soon after its inception, he foresaw a way to make the PIRG idea work much better. He would open offices in other cities, where colleges were present. Students could identify issues to be addressed and work in conjunction with their local PIRG to take substantive action.

To finance his new PIRG-college system, he had a unique method—through allocation of student activity fees. The colleges pay for guest speakers and athletic facilities out of activity fees, so why not ask each college to collect an extra two to three dollars from each student and allow the money to be funneled to the PIRG? This would allow students full access to their own team of lawyers, who would serve the public cause. It seemed an ideal and a worthwhile elective action.

These additional fees are usually subject to a vote of the student body, but to avoid the bureaucracy, Nader devised a negative check-off option, meaning that students who didn't want to donate the necessary PIRG funds would have to take direct, prescribed action to get their money back. He saw this as no different from the fees students paid for athletic teams they did not support. If only a small majority of students opted to open PIRGs at their colleges, the funds collected by this negative check-off plan would keep each PIRG self-sufficient.

Funding was always a problem for the organizations that Nader created, even though he contributed nearly every dime he earned, holding back little for his own expenses, and he made considerable money. He had become a client of the American Program Bureau in 1966, an agency that also represented such celebrity speakers as feminist Gloria Steinem and renowned pediatrician and author, Dr. Benjamin Spock. Nader spent a great deal of time speaking at various functions and colleges around the country. By 1970, Nader was earning the top dollar for each speech— $3,000 (worth almost $14,000 in 2003).[17] In that same year, he began to speak on the value of PIRGs at each college he visited. Oregon seemed to be most receptive to Nader's ideas, and he has continued to have a substantial following in that state. The University of Oregon PIRG came up with an annual budget of around $150,000 and was able to hire six young lawyers for its staff.

Propagating the PIRG concept was easy. Nader would speak in a college town, advocating the use of a PIRG to affect change. Then, a team of two young lawyers from the original PIRG would follow Nader into the same town and speak specifically to that topic. The mere mention that they were of Nader's crew brought interested students, and they would explain the PIRG concept in detail. Eventually, because the PIRG lawyers were so busy handling cases, Nader hired professional organizers to spread the word, but they were paid the same low wages and $11 a day for expenses. Their usual accommodations were college dorm rooms and cafeteria food. Yet, this was a wise plan of action to remain close to those students they wanted to ignite.

By 1974, 22 states had PIRGs and almost half a million students were involved in the project. They researched and attacked such projects as elementary school dental care, prison conditions, and the cost of prescription drugs in Vermont, St. Louis, and North Carolina. Today, state PIRGs are more active than ever. In part, the U.S. PIRG's mission statement reads, "We uncover threats to public health and well-being and fight to end them, using the time-tested tools of investigative research, media exposés, grassroots organizing, advocacy and litigation,"—all techniques devised and used by Nader himself. Recent issues have been arctic drilling, toy safety, student aid, and clean cars. Nader takes no credit for these successes. He claims merely to have started the ball rolling.

However, the negative check-off option for funding these PIRGs has not stood the test of time. Many colleges and universities have declined this method. Some opt for positive check-off (students can check if they want to donate to the PIRG), direct lobbying at the student government level for funding, and old-fashioned canvassing for support. Even funding obstacles have not dampened enthusiasm for these organizations, and they mark Nader's first attempt at organizing on a grassroots level. The success of his venture continues.

WOE BE THE WHISTLE-BLOWERS

Back in Washington on January 30, 1971, Nader took up another crusade—that of whistleblowers, people who are willing to speak out on misdeeds in the workplace. He held another press conference, again at the Mayflower Hotel. Only a few months before, he had met A. Ernest Fitzgerald, a man regarded highly by some, but loathed by others. As a deputy for management systems under the assistant secretary of the Air Force, Fitzgerald discovered that the C-5A, a heavy-cargo transport being built by Lockheed Aircraft, was $2 billion over budget and testified to this effect on November 13, 1968, before Senator William Proxmire's Subcommittee on Economy in Government, though he had been pressured by superiors not to do so. Fitzgerald was pressured similarly when he testified again about another matter before the Joint Economic Committee.

Fitzgerald was relieved of his duties and given trivial projects to oversee in countries far away. His colleagues shunned him, and he lost his civil service tenure, through a supposed "computer error." By November 4, 1969, Fitzgerald learned that his job was phased out because of a restructuring and reduction in force and he was fired, an action for which then President Richard M. Nixon took responsibility. Fitzgerald made an appeal to the Civil Service Commission, and in September 1973, the commission recommended that Fitzgerald be reinstated. Although Fitzgerald sued Nixon in civil court, the Supreme Court's 1981 opinion was that the president was immune from damages. Fitzgerald had spent some $900,000 in legal fees for his reinstatement.

At the 1971 press conference, in addition to Fitzgerald, who was a reluctant media star, was Jacqueline Verrett, an FDA scientist who discovered the cancer-causing elements in the artificial sweetener cyclamate; Ralph Stein, an Army intelligence officer who had uncovered the practice of putting civilians under surveillance; and A. Dale Console, former medical director at Squibb, who had blown the whistle for spurious practices by drug companies that led to doctors over- prescribing certain drugs. Nader delivered the keynote speech and said, "The key question is, at what point should an employee resolve that allegiance to society (e.g., the public safety) must supersede allegiance to the organization's policies (e.g., the corporate profit), and then act on that resolve by informing outsiders or legal authorities?"[18]

However, Nader did not advocate going outside the regular chain of command to bring these situations to light. He told the crowd that they first had to try to resolve problems from the inside, to pay attention to details, and when all else failed, to take their complaint to the people via the media. To aid in the process, Nader established the Clearinghouse for Professional Responsibility with Peter Petkas, a 25-year-old University of Texas law school graduate. Robert Townsend (father of Claire Townsend, who had helped in the Maiden Muckraker cause) and Stewart Mott, a General Motors heir who had supported Campaign GM, helped fund the effort.

Business was not enamored with Nader's recent cause. Recruiting whistle-blowers was not in their interests, and detractors labeled the Clearinghouse the "fink tank."[19] On hearing the criticism, Nathra Nader commented, "Something is very wrong in any government where the easiest way to lose your job is to do your job."[20]

NOTES

1. Nader had smoked about three-fourths of a pack a day until 1961, when he learned of the inherent health dangers in smoking tobacco, and since that time has been strongly anti-smoking.

2. Lallie Lloyd, interview with the author, 31 October 2003.

3. Lloyd, interview with the author, 31 October 2003.

4. Lloyd, interview with the author, 31 October 2003.

5. "Ralph Nader, Consumer Crusader, Interview," *The Academy of Achievement*, 16 February 1991, http://www.achievement.org/autodoc/page/nad0int-3.

6. Byron Bloch, interview with the author, 13 May 2004.

7. Byron Bloch, interview with the author, 13 May 2004.

8. Quoted in Justin Martin, *Nader, Crusader, Spoiler, Icon* (New York: Perseus, 2002), p. 107.

9. Richard Rowe, "Interview with Richard B. Smith," Securities and Exchange Commission Historical Society, 19 June 2000, http://www.sechistorical. org/museum/Museum_Papers/Archive_Paper_PDFs/Smith_Interview_JUN_19_02.pdf.

10. "Consumer Affairs: SEC Order to GM; Other Developments." *Facts on File World News Digest*, FACTS.com, 8 April 1970. http://www.2facts.com.

11. Quoted in Charles McCarry, *Citizen Nader* (New York: Saturday Review Press, 1972), p. 38.

12. Rose B. Nader and Nathra Nader, *It Happened in the Kitchen. Recipes for Food and Thought* (Washington, D.C.: Center for Study of Responsive Law, 1991), p. 172.

13. Lloyd, interview with the author, 31 October 2003.

14. "U.S. News: GM Settles with Nader." *Facts on File World News Digest*, FACTS.com, 19 August, 1970. http://www.2facts.com.

15. Samuel H. Williamson, "What is the Relative Value?" *Economic History Services*, April 2002, http://www.eh.net/hmit/compare/.

16. Williamson, "What is the Relative Value?"

17. Williamson, "What is the Relative Value?"

18. Quoted in Martin, *Nader, Crusader, Spoiler, Icon*, p. 135.

19. Quoted in Martin, *Nader, Crusader, Spoiler, Icon*, p. 137.

20. Nader and Nader, *It Happened in the Kitchen. Recipes for Food and Thought*, p. 160.

Chapter 6

THE CRUSADE GOES AWRY

In the early part of twenty-first century, Microsoft settled cases involving antitrust violations after many years of battling in the courts, though the company admitted no wrongdoing, and the media exposure has brought antitrust to the forefront of American current events. In 1970, however, this was not the case. Wondering why outraged citizens were not taking advantage of antitrust laws to stop companies from price-fixing, engaging in anticompetitive practices, monopolizing the market, and other violations of antitrust laws, Ralph Nader decided to launch the Nader Study Group on Antitrust Law Enforcement. Mark Green, a 25-year-old who had recently graduated from Harvard Law School, headed the nine-member task force.[1]

Green led the group to produce *The Closed Enterprise System*, published on January 1, 1972. The book disclosed the committee's findings, including information about how the 200 largest corporations were controlling two-thirds of all manufacturing assets in 1970, which resulted in a $60 billion loss in the gross national product. As normal practice, Nader wrote the book's introduction with a blazing first sentence and his wonderfully dry sense of humor, "This is a report on crime in the suites."[2] The actions of the Justice Department and, once again, the FTC were considered while the group studied the issues. The study group recommended creation of a new agency. "We conclude that a consolidation of the antitrust functions of the FTC and the Antitrust Division [of the Justice Department] into a unified new administrative agency—the Competition Protection Agency—would serve both good government and good antitrust enforcement.[3] The suggestion was never acted upon. The report also rec-

ommended that the mega corporations be split, with a savings to consumers of 25 percent in prices alone.

These disclosures had the book quickly climbing to #1 on the *New York
Times* bestseller list, and Nader saw the potential for consumer interest in
the topic. In 1971, he founded the Corporate Accountability Research
Group (CARG), directed by Green, and its task was to study corporate
power in relation to antitrust legislation. Several books came from this organization, such as *The Monopoly Makers* by Nader and Green and *Corporate Power in America,* edited by Nader and Green.

Nader and Green spent five years on the topic, culminating in the publication of an article for *Business and Society Review* and a book. The article, entitled "Who Rules the Giant Corporation?" was published in the
summer of 1976. Nader and Green blamed many spurious corporate practices on corporate chief executive officers: "The common theme of these
many instances of mismanagement is a failure to restrain the power of senior executives."[4] Nader and Green accused upper management of "proxy
soliciting" and urged shareholders to return proxies and to vote for their
chosen candidate. Average shareholders are not concerned with the
workings of upper management, so they tend to vote for a candidate
whose representative makes the effort to talk with them. The article
ended by blaming chartering states, "As business corporations have
evolved these new forms, Delaware and other principal chartering states
have deliberately not kept pace."[5]

The book emanating from the Nader-Green studies was *Taming the
Giant Corporation: How the Largest Corporations Control Our Lives,* with
co-author Joel Seligman in 1976. The book proposed federal chartering
for corporations, taking the process away from the states. The authors
stated, "In our view, the issue is whether the competitive enterprise system can be made to work equitably and efficiently. Federal chartering can
help attain this end. Grounded in competition and the Constitution, federal chartering is easily compatible with the principles that are supposed
to govern our society and economy."[6] The plan, however, was not received well by the business community, who likened the proposal to fas-
cism.

No matter how many projects Nader started, his vendetta against General Motors (GM) would not stop. He was irate, not only because of GM's
surveillance of him, but because he was convinced that GM executives
knew there were flaws in the Corvair's design, but sold it anyway. He continued to send letters to newspapers, to other consumer advocates, and
government officials. He also continued to beleaguer Senator Abraham

A. Ribicoff. Nader wrote to the *Washington Post* and complained that Ribicoff had written the Corvair and GM off.

Again, Ribicoff was infuriated by Nader's remarks. The first rebuke regarding the EPA had been confusing, but auto safety was Ribicoff's trademark. He had been known as "Mr. Auto Safety" when governor of Connecticut because of his backing of strict laws regarding drunken driving and speeding on Connecticut highways. Yet, Nader continued to harangue him in a series of lengthy, often technical letters.

POKING AT GM—AGAIN

Ribicoff ultimately acted when Nader asserted that GM executives had lied in their testimony to the Ribicoff subcommittee. Such a serious allegation had to be investigated, and Ribicoff set Robert Wager and John Koskinen on the project, using leads provided by Nader and Gary Sellers. Wager and Koskinen would determine if the executives knew of the dangers of Corvairs for consumers, lied to the subcommittee about passenger security in Corvair, yet sold them to unsuspecting consumers anyway.

The investigators did not come up with the conclusion Nader expected. The deeper they delved, the stronger was the evidence that the Corvair may have had handling problems under certain conditions, but that GM executives had no prior knowledge of these problems and they did not recklessly endanger the lives of those who purchased Corvairs. The 30,000-word account of their report was entered into the *Congressional Record* on March 27, 1973.

During the investigation, Nader had begun another Herculean project. He had undertaken to analyze and describe the workings of Congress, but at the level of each individual representative and senator, rather than at a general level. Nader felt them to be out of touch with real issues, and in the *New Republic*, he wrote "Making Congress Work," which appeared on August 21, 1971. He asserted that Congress was inundated with special interest lobbying and that the legislature should be improved and made more responsive to their constituent's needs.

The initial attack brought jeers from senators and representatives, who considered this Nader's retaliation for losing on the Consumer Protection Agency and most recently, the battle with GM. With his attacks on Muskie and Ribicoff, senators and representatives were less likely to become involved in Nader's causes. Of course, Nader was not pleased about the situation, but he had come to believe that trying to get legislation with teeth passed was impossible anyway. He felt that all the bills he had collaborated on were so watered-down by the time they became law that they were virtually useless.

BOON OR FIASCO?

Now, Nader was going in another direction. He attacked Congress at the roots and during a luncheon at the National Press Club on November 2, 1971, he announced the "Congress Project," which would delve into the records surrounding 484 members of Congress, who were up for re-election. Nader also announced that the money to fund the project would come from his own pocket and that results would be made public in the autumn of 1972, just in time for voters to make educated choices. He named Robert C. Fellmeth as the project's director.

To complete the crew, a dozen other Raiders were signed up to assist in the project, including Joan Claybrook. The daughter of a Baltimore City Councilman, Claybrook spent her undergraduate years at Goucher College and then went to work for the Social Security Administration. In 1966, she was involved in auto safety legislation through Congressman James Mackay of Georgia. Claybrook also worked for the National Highway Safety Bureau (NHSB). During this time, she first met Nader. Claybrook earned a law degree from Georgetown in 1970, became part of the Public Interest Research Group (PIRG) project, and ultimately became one of the most influential and vital elements of the entire Nader organization.

Nader intended to supplement his Congress Project core crew with 1,000 Raiders, whom he would hire in the summer of 1972.

While this preliminary work was in progress, Nader recognized a need to fund his other projects because he planned to dump all his earned speaking income to the Congress Project. Of the roughly $250,000 a year he made speaking, Nader continued to keep only $5,000 a year for himself. About the time he was organizing the projects he intended to carry his organization into 1972, he founded Public Citizen as a nonprofit organization, funded by donations from the public.

Nader used the media to obtain the donations, as he had used the media to fuel his projects. On October 31, 1971, Nader took out ads in the *Washington Post* and the *New York Times*, asking that consumers take action. His letters began, "Dear Fellow Citizen, Imagine that 25 or 30 years ago citizens concerned about the future quality of life in America had gotten together to do something about it."[7] In the first year, Public Citizen garnered $1.1 million.

With this influx of funding, Nader organized more groups, such as the Health Research Group, the Corporate Accountability Research Group

(CARG), the Tax Reform Research Group, the Center for Auto Safety, and Public Citizen Litigation Group (which would eventually replace the original PIRG), among others. Though Nader left the internal workings of each group to their members, he continued to oversee their actions and to sign each member's paycheck.

Nader had been high profile for several years on his own. Now, he was in charge, even if only loosely, of a burgeoning consumer protection machine. The people were behind him. When Fellmeth asked for volunteers for Ralph Nader's Congress Project, several hundred stepped forward. They would gather the needed data to profile each member of Congress's voting district.

THE *WAR AND PEACE* OF QUESTIONNAIRES

Fellmeth was busy putting together a tome-like 96-page questionnaire that each representative and senator who was being studied was asked to complete, and it included policy statements on many sensitive issues. The group wanted to lay the groundwork for the new Raiders who would join the team that summer. They would be expected to conduct interviews with members of Congress and to write each evaluation they were assigned. Grossman, which had published many of the Nader reports and *Unsafe at Any Speed,* would be available for publishing their reports.

Obtaining the needed manpower to complete the project would be easy, since applications flooded into the Nader organizations each summer, mainly from students in prestigious colleges or recent graduates, many of them law students or new lawyers. For those who would be report writers, Fellmeth required a personal interview, but for other legwork employees, they simply pulled resumes from a pile, as though they were selecting lottery winners.

The Congress Project employees would receive only $500 for the entire summer's work, but the people involved were more interested in changing government and the stepping-stone that working for Nader would provide. George Washington University offered its dorms as accommodations for the workers, but room and board would be deducted from their pay. Volunteers were always welcome.

Orientation was held for the Congress Project participants on June 3, 1972, at a George Washington University dorm, where Nader stated to his audience that the Congress Project would surpass anything a Nader group had ever done before. He also cautioned the group to avoid smoking marijuana, as any repercussions would reflect badly on the group, and he gave them a Labor Day deadline.

The Congress Project people found this deadline to be impossible. Many members of Congress refused to cooperate, uninterested in being dragged over the coals by the Nader contingent. Some were gracious and answered whatever they were asked—vaguely. The general attitude was one of intense loathing of the picayune scrutiny. The voluminous survey was not winning enthusiasm, either. Answering 633 questions takes a very long time. Sixty-three members refused to answer any questions in any form. That did not exempt them from being profiled, however, as the report writers just used previously published materials for reference.

Fifty of the new Raiders were chosen to write the profiles, and each writer had to write 9 profiles of approximately 30 pages each. Sources had to be footnoted, and the manuscripts typewritten. There were no word processors or computers, and when they made copies of their work, they were asked to use carbon paper until the copies from it were no longer legible.

Claybrook, who supervised the writing staff, advised the young people that their already meager pay would be docked $50 for each profile not done. Claybrook and other members of the core staff were appalled that the writers sometimes asked elementary questions about the workings of Congress. To have been a college student or worse, a college graduate, and not know about Congress was an anathema to the core group of Nader's Raiders, and they tended to look at the questioners with contempt. The dynamics of the group began to deteriorate.

DISSENTION AND REBELLION

The writers called a private meeting to discuss the issues, without supervisors; however, Claybrook heard about the session and showed up. The writers complained about losing money if they could not complete all the work, though they were working as hard as they possibly could. They also lamented that writing about some no-name, no-accomplishment representatives and senators proved to be quite difficult. Claybrook listened and agreed to relay the information to Nader.

When Nader heard that the writers were restless, he called another meeting and gave them a pep talk. Then, he extended their deadline by one week and lowered the number of profiles they were required to write from nine to eight. To alleviate the workload, he also agreed to hire freelance writers to take up the slack.

Amid the confusion, George McGovern contacted Nader in early August and asked Nader to run as his vice president in the 1972 presidential election. Yet, Nader declined. At that point, he did not intend to become a candidate himself, let alone one aligned with either the Democratic or the Republican Party. He had promised his father to remain independent. Nathra always said, "When asked whether I am a Republican or a Democrat, I reply that I am an American."[8] He abhorred the two-party system in America and thought that both parties represented the same special interests. His son supported those views.

Aside from having no interest in becoming a politician, Nader was too embroiled in the Congress Project to run. As the time became shorter and the project was still a long way from completion, he decided to put out a small paperback about the study, something to whet the public's appetite for the complete reports. Mark Green was its primary author.

This action infuriated the report writers, who felt the book would steal the import of their hard work over the entire summer. They thought the public would prefer this synopsis, rather than their detailed data, and Nader seemed to be promoting the book because he had lost faith in them. Some threatened to quit; others vowed to withhold information from the book authors.

Nader called another meeting on August 8 in which he became quite forthright. He told those that wanted to quit to do so and the others to get on with the work. He reminded them that he knew how to use the media and that it was important to give the public the idea that the reports, which were full of pertinent data but quite dry, were vital to making a concerned voting choice. He told them that those who did not trust his judgment could leave and left the podium.

Who Runs Congress? by Mark Green with Michael Calabrese was written in six weeks and edited in one day. It hit the bestseller lists, but was not well received by critics. *Time* magazine said it was full of errors, and a Knight-Ridder review called it combative.

THE CONGRESS PROJECT: SUCCESS OR WASTE?

At last, the profiles were completed and they were massive, but the public did not get to see them until October 22, 1972. Distribution was another complication because the group had to be sure to get the right profiles into the right markets. Reviewers, once again, were not enthused. The *New York Times* claimed that these reports gave no new information. The *Denver Post* asked how Nader's group could claim it was the most authoritative study of Congress when there were so many errors. The entire project cost Nader $500,000.

Regarding its success, Nader said,

It's hard to measure what kind of impact it had; its impact was that no one had ever done that before. People had in their hands a magazine-size report on each member of Congress running for reelection. There's no way to measure. I know it irritated quite a few and they fought back and put out statements, so it didn't just glide over the election.

It created controversy in the press and in [Congressional] districts. We had regional press conferences as well as a Washington press conference to release the reports at the same time all over the country, but it basically told incumbents that from now on, there was going to be more attention to their record. While it was never done again, the very fact that it could have been done obviously was on their minds.[9]

Nader sees all projects in a positive light. If they accomplish anything at all, they are worthwhile. So, he never stopped. Nader looked for causes, and it was not hard to find them. After fighting the antitrust business with GM throughout 1973, he took on nuclear energy and the public's right to view federal information.

MORE VENUES FOR ACTION

The Freedom of Information Act (FOIA) became law on July 4, 1966, and was seen as potential advancement in the democratic process. However, the original act featured nine exceptions, including records of ongoing investigations, documents pertaining to the national security, and personnel files; however, the exceptions were not mandatory. Each individual agency was able to develop its own policy regarding the exceptions. Nader saw these exceptions as wide loopholes that favored the government and accused the act of shielding information from public access. He laid out these thoughts in the article "Freedom from Information," which was published that year in the *Harvard Law Review*.

In conjunction with his outrage over the blatant attempts to undermine the law, Nader founded the Freedom of Information Clearinghouse in 1972, as an arm of the Public Citizen Litigation Group. The Clearinghouse distributed information about the public's right to scrutinize government documents, with the Litigation group standing by to fight breeches of the law. Most often, their cases involved journalists or academic researchers who were denied information.

One case involved Carl Stern, a television journalist, who wanted records concerning J. Edgar Hoover's project to investigate leftists. When the FBI refused to give the information on the bureau's war on dissidents in America, Stern went to his employer, who refused to wage a lengthy and costly legal battle. So, Stern approached Nader, whose Public Citizen lawyers were ready, more than willing, and able to take up his cause. Stern's lawyers won the case, and the documents released contained the first information released to confirm the "Cointelpro—New Left" operation.

This free access to government information was important to Nader, as was the question of nuclear energy, which he had begun to investigate in 1970, when he undertook an intensive study of the Atomic Energy Commission (AEC) with the University of Texas *Law Review*. In a 1998 interview with *PBS: Frontline*, Nader said, "This was a time of maximum energy waste in the early '70s before the so-called oil embargo. And we thought the mere investment in energy efficiency would replace far more than the megawatts that could be supplied by risky nuclear power."[10] Nader saw the risks as much worse than the benefits. "It became clear that nuclear power was too hazardous, too costly, and unnecessary to provide electricity for our country."[11]

Nader read as much as he could about nuclear energy and became expert in the subject. He collected data from prominent scientists and interpreted it. What he found was not pleasing. Nuclear energy, Nader believed, was dangerous and inefficient, and his biggest complaint was that nuclear energy was not properly controlled.

To intensify his views on nuclear power, Nader held a conference entitled Critical Mass on November 16, 17, and 18, 1974, at the Statler Hilton in Washington, D.C. The gathering was intended to raise awareness of the dangers of nuclear energy and to brainstorm new energy alternatives. Several well-renowned and respected figures attended, including prominent ecologist Barry Commoner, anthropologist Margaret Mead, and actor Robert Redford. The name of the conference was another hint of Nader's wry sense of humor. Critical mass is the least amount of a fissional material needed to sustain a nuclear chain reaction at a constant level—in this case, the number of dedicated people needed to gain action and results. Participants were thrilled to see that their own grassroots organizations could join with other antinuclear groups and make their voices heard. To supplement these activities, Nader created a new organization and labeled it Critical Mass. Another Critical Mass conference would be held on November 13, 1975, on the anniversary of Karen Silkwood's death.

MERE TRAGEDY OR MURDER?

Silkwood was an employee of the Kerr-McGee Corporation at the Cimarron River plant near Crescent, Oklahoma, and her story was immortalized in the film *Silkwood*, starring Meryl Streep. Silkwood was a member of the Oil, Chemical, and Atomic Workers' Union, and a week before her death was secretly gathering information about safety issues at the plant for the union to present as a grievance against the company.

On November 5, she was found to have plutonium-239 from the metallography laboratory on her hands. In the Glove Box lab, where employees work through glove ports inside a radiation-safe box, she had been polishing plutonium pellets, used in fuel rods. The right side of her body was also contaminated. At the plant's Health Physics office, she was given a nasal "swipe," to measure airborne plutonium pollution, which was moderately positive. She was decontaminated with ethylene diamine tetra acetic acid (EDTA) soap, which can be damaging to the skin and to the mucous membranes of the eyes and nose. Silkwood also underwent testing of her urine and feces for five days to determine plutonium levels in her body.

The following day, she did not work in the Glove Box, but she was again found to be contaminated and had to undergo the same treatments as the day before. When she turned in a few days' worth of samples of her bodily wastes, extremely high levels of activity were found. Her car and locker were checked, but the results were negative. When her home was examined, low levels of plutonium were found everywhere. Still, it was determined that the cumulative amount of 300 micrograms was not dangerous to her health or to others with whom she would come into contact.

On November 11, Silkwood met with Dr. George Voelz, head of the health laboratory division of the company, along with a roommate and her boyfriend, who were also to be checked for radiation. Although her friends tested positive for small amounts, Silkwood was found to have significant plutonium levels in her lungs, but was assured that she would not develop cancer and that she could have normal children. Her levels were still below acceptable amounts.

Silkwood was no longer permitted to work with radiation. She attended a union meeting on November 13, and on her way home, died in a one-car accident. She was purportedly on her way to meet a *New York Times* reporter and an official from the AEC with documents to prove her allegations of inadequate safety precautions by the company. Speculation has surrounded her death ever since.

During the autopsy, Silkwood was found to have high levels of the euphoria-producing and now legally banned medication methaqualone, and her death was pronounced a typical sleepy driver mishap. No documents were found in her car. Silkwood's estate filed suit against Kerr-McGee for inadequate safety precautions and eventually settled out of court for $1.3 million. Her case raised even more questions about corporate responsibility and the dangers of nuclear energy.

By 1973, however, Nader was back with an old cause and another new organization—Congress Watch, headed by Claybrook. This Nader arm fought many antinuclear lobbying battles with members of Congress. Nader and Claybrook also opposed metal breeder reactors. These use plutonium as fuel, which can be reused infinitely—much longer than uranium—and which degrades over time. Congress Watch helped build a solid lobby against breeder reactors, and ultimately, Congress stopped funding these projects in 1983.

FOIA proved a valuable instrument for Congress Watch, as well. Even the PIRGs were involved in the fight against the proliferation of nuclear power. Nader rallied all the troops in this cause, which appears to have been successful. The last nuclear power plant was opened in 1988; no new plants have been opened. Though the Naderites had considerable influence, they were not the sole reason for the halt in building new plants, which are very expensive. Still, public opinion had deteriorated regarding nuclear power because of Nader and his groups' intervention, which undoubtedly made a lasting impression.

As 1974 ended, the presidential election had already begun to heat up and Nader had made some lasting impressions himself. People had continued to urge him to run for the office. Yet, Nader had refused in the past and would continue to eschew political life. He was not interested in becoming involved in politics. His man that year would be Jimmy Carter, who vowed at an August 9, 1975, luncheon, sponsored by Public Citizen, that he hoped to challenge Nader as the nation's top consumer advocate. Nader felt that perhaps the president would finally be in his corner.

NOTES

1. Green continued to work for Nader for 10 years and then became New York City's consumer affairs commissioner. After 12 years in that position, he was elected as the city's first public advocate. He ran in the 2001 mayoral election in New York City, but lost to Michael Bloomberg.

2. Mark J. Green, with Beverly C. Moore, Jr., and Bruce Wasserstein, "Introduction" by Ralph Nader, *The Closed Enterprise System, Ralph Nader's Study Group Report on Antitrust Enforcement*. (New York: Grossman, 1972), p. ix.

3. Green, Moore, and Wasserstein, *The Closed Enterprise System, Ralph Nader's Study Group Report on Antitrust Enforcement*, p. 433.

4. Ralph Nader, *The Ralph Nader Reader* (New York: Seven Stories Press, 2000), p. 115.

5. Nader, *The Ralph Nader Reader*, p. 127.

6. Ralph Nader, Mark Green, and Joel Seligman, *Taming the Giant Corporation: How the Largest Corporations Control Our Lives* (New York: W. W. Norton, 1976), p. 263.

7. Quoted in de Toledano, *Hit and Run, the Rise–And Fall?–of Ralph Nader*, p. 9.

8. Rose B. Nader and Nathra Nader, *It Happened in the Kitchen. Recipes for Food and Thought* (Washington, D.C.: Center for Study of Responsive Law, 1991), p. 169.

9. Ralph Nader, interview with the author, 15 August 2003.

10. "Interview with Ralph Nader, Nuclear Reaction, Why Do Americans Fear Nuclear Power?" *PBS: Frontline*, http://www.pbs.org/wgbh/pages/frontline/shows/reaction/interviews/nader.html.

11. "Interview with Ralph Nader, Nuclear Reaction."

Young Ralph Nader with his sister Laura. (Courtesy of Claire Nader)

(above) Ralph Nader,
approximately 9–10 years
old, and friend with pro-
duce from a victory garden
during WWII. (Courtesy
of Claire Nader)

(right) Ralph Nader posing
with his mother, Rose.
(Courtesy of Claire
Nader)

Ralph Nader on a wintery day. (Courtesy of Claire Nader)

Ralph Nader as a teenager. (Courtesy of Claire Nader)

Ralph Nader outlined his ideas on the democratic uses of science and technology before a standing-room-only audience of Lawrence Berkeley Laboratory staff members at an Environmental Science Seminar in the auditorium, 1971. (Courtesy of the Lawrence Berkeley National Laboratory)

Ralph Nader, the Green Party's expected candidate for president, listens to a reporter's question at a news conference, July 27, 1996, in Berkeley, California. (AP/WIDE WORLD PHOTOS)

With the New York Stock Exchange in the background, Ralph Nader, right, addresses a crowd from the steps of New York's Federal Hall, October 4, 2002, during a rally promoting honest business and protecting workers' pensions. (AP/WIDE WORLD PHOTOS)

Presidential hopeful Ralph Nader addresses a news conference at the National Press Club in Washington, February 23, 2004. (AP/WIDE WORLD PHOTOS)

Chapter 7

LOSING HIS LUSTER

Rumblings in the press urged Nader to run for president during the 1976 presidential campaign; however, he was not interested in becoming president and did not see himself as a politician but, rather, as an influencer of politicians, more like a kingmaker. Jimmy Carter boosted Ralph Nader's view when he invited Nader to meet with him in his hometown of Plains, Georgia, on August 7 and 8, 1976, before Carter spoke at the Public Citizen meeting on August 9. After their Georgia conference, Nader said that Carter's views were "a breath of fresh air,"[1] and on his first night in Plains, Nader even umpired a baseball game between teams headed by Carter and his brother Billy.

Nader and Carter discussed much that weekend—much of what Carter related to the Public Citizen gathering. He proposed to make it illegal for government regulators to come from the very industries they were intended to regulate. He also came out against nuclear power and promised to dramatically cut back budgeting for breeder reactors. Though Carter opposed Nader's plan to break up major oil companies, he did pledge to make federal regulatory appointments based on Nader's recommendations.

By October, the Ford campaign was telling voters, "If you want Ralph Nader in the White House, vote for Jimmy Carter."[2] The Republicans, with their strong business-oriented constituency, were hostile to Nader and his consumer movement. As things heated up, the Naderites worried that Carter would lose the election. The previous Republican administrations of Richard M. Nixon and Gerald R. Ford had ignored the consumer issues and their supporters, and those in the consumer movement believed that Ford's election would be a devastating blow because it would mean four more years of the same Republican stonewalling. Joan Clay-brook said, "I think I would recommend disbanding Congress Watch and move to grass roots organizing. It's impossible to always have to be faced with the need of getting two-thirds of Congress to support you because you know a veto is coming."[3]

Luckily for the Naderites, the election turned out as they had hoped, and Jimmy Carter won the presidency by a narrow majority. At least they thought it was a lucky break. Carter was Nader's man, after all. Yet, what they had not counted on was Carter's penchant for being a pleaser. He wanted to cater to both sides to keep peace, so there were bound to be happy victories and bad feelings on both sides.

The month before Carter took the oath of office, Nader criticized him for reneging on his promise to consult Nader regarding appointments to cabinet level positions, which he had agreed to do while Nader was in Georgia. Nader was most concerned about Carter's appointment of attorney general, as he was anxious to have antitrust legislation enforced and had people in mind who would view Nader's stance as positive. Carter did appoint Joan Claybrook as head of the National Highway and Transportation Administration and James Fallows as his chief speechwriter. Peter Petkas joined the Office of Management and Budget (OMB) and Harrison Wellford, past executive director of the Center for the Study of Responsive Law, was named the OMB's executive associate director. Many other posts were filled, not by ex-Raiders, but by people involved in or sympathetic to the consumer movement. Carol Tucker Forsman, former executive director of the Consumer Federation of America, the nation's largest consumer lobbying group, was named assistant secretary of Agriculture of consumer and nutrition services. And Peter Schuck, an attorney for the Consumer's Union, became deputy assistant secretary for planning and evaluation in the Department of Housing and Urban Development.

On the big business side of the fence, heavy industry was disappointed in Carter's consideration of Arthur Fox for secretary of Labor. Fox was former secretary under President Ford, and they felt his interests lay in maintaining the status quo in labor. Both sides were unhappy, so Carter's administration started with an air of distrust. Author and political analyst David Brian Robertson wrote, "The collective impression that Carter's appointees gave was one of an irresolute leader who was eager to accommodate all sides. Carter never seemed to be in control of events, but his weaknesses were not merely attributable to his personal inadequacies; rather, they were symptomatic of the crisis in the liberal order."[4]

Nader's disapproval of Carter's actions began to show up with Nader's appearance as guest host of *Saturday Night Live* on January 15, 1977, just days before Carter was to be sworn in as the 39th president of the United States. Comedienne Gilda Radner worried that Nader might be too straight for the show, but he came onto the set wearing a powder blue cowboy suit, complete with fringe and a kerchief, an appearance diametrically opposed to the perception the American public had of him, with his trademark rumpled black suits, white shirts, and black shoes and tie. Though resuming his normal attire following the opening skit, Nader continued to poke fun at his consumer-oriented ideals and at his relationship with Jimmy Carter, starting to go wrong. "Oh Carter!" he said in one sketch. "What a cabinet! I wonder if he cares what I think now that the election is over?"[5]

THE MAIN TOPIC—ENERGY

Carter's main thrust at the beginning of his term in office was comprehensive energy legislation. In 1973, a severe gasoline shortage had frustrated consumers, who sometimes waited hours in long lines at gas pumps only to find the pumps dry when it was their turn to fuel up. This shortage began shortly after the advent of the Yom Kippur War in the Middle East between Arab States and Israel on October 6, 1973. In retaliation for the United States siding with Israel, the Organization of Petroleum Exporting Countries (OPEC) placed an embargo on the oil it had been exporting to America.

Though the United States had relied on its own stores of oil in the 1950s, oil usage had risen because of the proliferation of automobiles, trucks, and airplanes. Oil was also used in fertilizer, synthetic materials, and even drugs. At the time, OPEC called the embargo, the United States was importing 35 percent of the country's oil consumption. To heighten the issue, OPEC raised prices by 70 percent so that a gallon of gasoline went from 38 cents to more than one dollar, until the embargo was dropped on March 18, 1974.

Several measures to alleviate the need for imported oil took effect during that time. President Nixon had a 55-mile-an-hour speed limit imposed, stopped the sale of gasoline on Sundays, and asked station owners to limit sales to customers to ten gallons each. He also extended daylight savings time and asked Americans to conserve energy by lowering thermostats and by turning off lights and appliances when not using them. Congress also approved the construction of the Alaskan pipeline, which would supply 2,000,000 barrels of oil a day, although this would not be completed until 1977.

Obviously, these measures were stopgaps, but the crisis continued into the administration of President Ford, who took office on August 9, 1974, after President Nixon resigned following the Watergate scandal.[6] On October 11, Ford signed the Energy Reorganization Act of 1974, which abolished the Atomic Energy Commission (AEC). The Energy Research and Development Administration and the Nuclear Regulatory commission replaced the AEC. Ford also formed the Energy Resources Council, which would be his new board, with its only function as structuring a formal department for energy and natural resources, at which time it would terminate. Ford was determined to take steps to see that the energy crisis did not come about again.

During the presidential campaign of 1976, both Ford and Carter supported steps to cure the nation's energy problems. Yet, America did not see energy as a major issue. They continued to blame OPEC's embargo and a conspiracy among oil companies to raise prices for these shortages, which they believed to be only temporary. The winter of 1976 to 1977 turned bitterly cold, and energy sources found it hard to meet demands in some parts of the country. In New England, where natural gas supplies fell far short of the demand, companies closed or shortened working hours for the duration of the cold snap, and thousands of school children were given surprise extended vacations. When Carter was inaugurated, the public looked to him for a solution.

Carter's first action was to proclaim a national emergency in the Natural Gas Act of 1977. In one of his fireside chats, where he would appear on camera in a cardigan sweater sitting beside a fire, he asked Americans to conserve energy once again and promised to present a comprehensive energy plan to Congress by mid-April. He described each American's obligation to conserve energy as the "moral equivalent to war."[7] He met the deadline on March 1.

A COMPLICATED ROAD TO FRUITION

As presented to Speaker of the House Tip O'Neill, Carter's energy plan came as five phone-book-sized volumes. At the Department of Energy's history site on the World Wide Web, the plan was described thusly: "Carter's National Energy Plan consisted of approximately 100 proposals ranging from administrative actions to new laws and regulations. The plan placed heavy emphasis on reducing energy consumption, implementing conservation, and developing alternative energy technologies."[8] Through this plan, Carter hoped that the reduction of consumption, increased coal productivity, and the use of solar energy in homes and businesses wherever possible, would decrease the demand for energy in the United States, though the country would still not be energy independent. He intended to make the resources we had stretch farther by using less.

After looking the proposals over, O'Neill knew that it would have to be examined and reexamined by committees and subcommittees and opposing opinions would water the measure down so heavily that it would never get off the ground. To avoid the boondoggle, he formed an ad hoc committee to fully consider Carter's proposals, and by June 3, the House passed the legislation.

The Senate, also working on the legislation, had no catchall ad hoc committee and what O'Neill feared for the legislation in the house happened in the Senate committees and subcommittees. Fierce battles ensued, culminating in a filibuster by liberal senators, assuming they had the administration's best interests at heart. After so much chopping and changing, the proposed amendments had made Carter's bill unrecognizable. Still, Carter was the one to put an end to the first Senate filibuster in 13 years, without even notifying the Senators backing the administration. For this, he used Vice President Walter Mondale, who stepped in as presiding officer in the Senate, as is his constitutional right. He brought up a point of order, stating that some 500 amendments to the natural gas bill, which had been presented by the Senators supporting the Carter administration, were "dilatory," meaning they were irrelevant to the vote on the energy package, and therefore would not be considered any further. By doing this, he forced the vote and the resultant legislation was a severely weakened version of what the administration had intended in the beginning.

Senator Howard Metzenbaum of Ohio and Senator James Abourezk of South Dakota, who led the Democratic liberals in their fight, along with Senator Edward Kennedy of Massachusetts and Senator Birch Bayh of Indiana, were devastated by the actions of the very sponsors they were in league to support. "All I know is what I've been told from the beginning:...that all governments lie," Abourezk said. "But there is one thing that I thought would never happen, and that is that Jimmy Carter would lie."[9] Carter signed the new bill into law on August 4, 1977, thus creating the Department of Energy.

Carter's behavior in this matter incensed members of his own party, and he had held passage of the energy package as the mark of success for his first year in office. His inability to get Congress to support rebates on small car purchases or get a new gasoline tax passed, accompanied by his own capitulation in the Senate struggles, angered many, including Nader, who accused Carter of being a "sheep in wolf's clothing."[10] Carter responded by accusing the congressional representatives of being swayed by the big oil and auto lobbies.

DISAPPOINTMENT CONTINUES

Other areas of Carter's administration came under attack from Nader, and one was most surprising when he clamored for the resignation of Joan Claybrook as the head of the National Highway Traffic Safety Administration on November 30. He demanded that she acknowledge her ineffectiveness in the post and described her time in the post as a "trail of broken promises."[11] These statements were made in an 11-page letter, which in Nader's usual fashion, had been distributed to reporters before Claybrook ever saw it. Some of his statements were quite personal: "This is more than a failure of leadership; it is a failure of nerve."[12] He was most incensed that automobiles would not be required to have air bag protection for an additional four years, and he accused Claybrook of listening more to industry than to consumers. But this attack, in conjunction with those made on other consumer-oriented members of government was, he insisted, not personal. "The issues are bigger than that," he said.[13]

At a press conference to answer Nader's letter, Claybrook told reporters that she had favored a three-year limit on air bag requirements, but her superior, who wanted a four-year limit, overruled her. She also said that other safety standards were in the works, but had not yet been finalized.

About that time, Nader entered the room. When asked by another reporter how she felt about Nader's attack, she replied, "Not good."[14] It was noted that Nader put his head down and smiled. When he tried to ask her a question, she ignored him, saying she had held the press conference to talk to reporters, not to him. Their feud continued for years.

Nader also attacked Harrison Wellford at the OMB. Nader referred to him as a box shuffler, and Wellford was furious. Wellford asserted that once in politics, checks and balances take over, and nothing could be as simple as being on the outside. He claimed that no one could please Nader very long.

In 1978, a new group sprang up by the name of Consumers Opposed to Inflation in the Necessities (COIN). Led by Roger Hickey, who helped found the group in 1978, the organization's goal was alternative solutions to fighting inflation, which was at 7.6 percent that year and getting worse. In a report from the University of Notre Dame, the make-up and purpose of COIN was described: "During the years of the Carter Administration a broad-based coalition proposed that the 'necessities of life' be made the central thrust of an equitable anti-inflation program which could also help achieve sustained economic growth. More than 70 consumer, labor, environmental, senior-citizen, and minority organizations—Consumers Opposed to Inflation of the Necessities (COIN)—proposed policies to hold down price increases in the four key sectors."[15] Those sectors were food, shelter, energy, and medical costs. One might also include the need for clothing in that batch, and COIN and its constituents were most concerned with inflation in these arenas.

On December 19, 1978, representatives of COIN arranged to meet with President Carter to discuss his anti-inflation policies and programs. Since the interview had been so hard to attain, the team decided to carefully orchestrate each member's speech. Nader was part of that group, but when it came time for him to speak, he used the time for promoting his own agenda. The group was very unhappy and the meeting ended in just 23 minutes. Yet, it would not be the last meeting for the president and Nader, who would occasionally continue to speak on the telephone and at the White House.

QUEST FOR A CPA

The next battle that Nader waged was an old one—a push to create a suitable consumer protection agency (CPA). In April 1977, President Carter endorsed a new proposal and sent a message to Congress stating that the new agency was not intended to be regulatory, but only to improve the manner in which existing laws and regulations were enforced. He also endorsed a measure to allow consumers to file suit against big companies as a class (class-action lawsuits). In June, he declared that special-interest lobbyists had been zealously fighting the bill, and said that he saw the proposed agency as a means for consumers to have a voice in government, to oppose those of big business.

Robert J. Buckley, then Chairman of Allegheny Ludlum Industries, Inc., spoke at Fordham University on August 17, 1977, and made three points alerting the public to the dangers of consumerism:

1. America in 1977 is a different society from any on this continent in the 200 years of our history.
2. The "consumerism" movement in America is
   a. a current major social, economic, and political phenomenon that must not be ignored
   b. led by "activists," many of whose aims are to reorder society along an egalitarian, collectivist, anti-growth, anti-technology model.

3. The American form of government is in jeopardy if we suc-
cumb to "activists" pressures and allow increased government intervention and regulation of the private sector—in
the name of "consumer protection"...with serious consequences to your individual freedom.[16]

Buckley's comments were disturbing. Big business's view of consumerism had always been askew, but now the atmosphere was turning
negative in the public arena as well. Buckley also quoted Marjorie Boyd,
who wrote in the *Washington Monthly*,

Many congressmen who previously supported the idea of a
Consumer Protection Agency were surprised earlier this year
to find opposition to the bill growing among their constituents—congressmen are increasingly hearing from the ad-
visers and friends who serve as political barometers in their
districts that people are not so keen on consumer legislation as
they once were. The bill suffered a severe blow when a recent
convention of the Federated American Women's Clubs passed
a resolution opposing the consumer agency.[17]

Buckley cited the placement of Naderites in government as one reason
that the public was concerned. He stated that they disliked the idea of
government regulation. He also mentioned Nader's nickel campaign, saying the idea went too far.

In June 1977, Nader was embroiled in a vigorous push to get the Consumer Protection Agency through Congress and on to the president's
desk. He came up with the idea of getting consumers to mail a nickel to
congressional representatives who opposed the bill, since that would be
the cost to each American for establishment of the agency. For a few
months, nickels flooded the offices of senators and representatives who
would not back the legislation. The torrent of 43 thousand coins irritated
the congressional representatives, especially those who received coins and
were already in favor of the legislation.

Nader also set on a personal campaign in the hometowns of opposing
senators and representatives. He lambasted them in the press and on the
radio for not getting behind the new agency. It was no wonder that when
the Consumer Protection Agency bill was put on the agenda on February
8, 1978, it was defeated. Rather than the champion, as he had been
viewed in the past, this time Nader was seen as the spoiler.

However, Nader credits the demise of the bill to President Carter. They had met in the Oval Office the previous month, and Nader had given the president a list of members of Congress who were undecided about their vote concerning the CPA. Carter was to phone each of them and try to persuade them to vote affirmatively. Yet, Carter had called only six and then stopped, as the reactions to all his calls were negative. Carter was dealing with other issues at the time, and the lack of enthusiasm in Congress for the CPA sent his efforts toward the issue spiraling downward.

It seemed that Congress had tired of Nader. His tactics began to grate on nerves and his great plans for the Carter administration were dissolving. He also lost the easy pipeline to the press. With the Watergate scandals and the prominence of reporters Bob Woodward and Carl Bernstein who uncovered the governmental conspiracy, reporters had taken to becoming investigators themselves instead of simply publishing the copy Nader provided. For the first time in more than a decade, Nader was being ignored.

THE PATH OF CONSUMER PROTECTION

He was not the only bee in the hive anymore, either. Consumer organizations sprang up around the country. In 1975, Robert Choate's Council on Children, Media and Merchandising found that 50 percent of the advertising on children's television programs came from the food industry and that the products were primarily sugared cereal, candy, cookies, and soft drinks. Council members also learned that 30 percent of advertising during children's programming was for toys. In 1977, the council released its complete study entitled *Edible TV: Your Child and Food Commercials*, which was prepared for the Senate Committee of Nutrition and Human Needs.

John Banzhaf III even followed Nader's lead by recruiting students to conduct investigations. They were referred to as Banzhaf's Bandits. Banzhaf has been called the Ralph Nader of the Tobacco Industry and the Ralph Nader of Junk Food. Banzhaf helped with legislation to get smoking commercials off the air, and in 1967, he founded Action on Smoking and Health (ASH). He was also behind action to sue former Vice President Spiro T. Agnew to recover the bribes he had received and for which he had resigned his office.

In 1966, Barry Commoner, a leading environmental activist founded the Center for the Biology of Natural Systems (CBNS), a research institute that studies the environmental impact of issues such as trash disposal, carcinogens, and agricultural pollution.

Yet, Nader was still at the forefront. The leaders of the new groups were the "Naders" in their field of interest, and their study groups were all patterned after the Nader plan. Their work came to the forefront of consumer and political attention at the same time as Nader battled one cause, then another, and the new groups tackled and often were victorious against important issues of the day. Yet, around 1978, Nader came up with a new action group—Fight to Advance the Nation's Sports (FANS), which was partially inspired by his lifelong love of baseball. Yet, the organization did more harm than good to Nader's already tarnished reputation.

FANS was intended to protest the inadequacies of our nation's ballparks, such as poor seating, bad hot dogs, warm beer, and overpriced tickets. Peter Gruenstein, an alumnus of the 1972 Congress Project, was in league with Nader on the project, and to get it started, Nader donated $10,000 of his own money.

The FANS campaign kicked off with an article in the March 1978 issue of *Playboy* magazine. Nader and Gruenstein co-authored the work, entitled "Fans: The Sorry Majority." The article outlined how fans were mistreated and proposed a fans' bill of rights. Yet, this new campaign was not well received by the media or the public. Reporters began to joke that Nader would start lobbying for air bags in football players' shoulder pads and spinach to be sold in stadiums, rather than hot dogs. FANS lasted only a short time and then faded.

A SUDDEN DECLINE IN POPULARITY

Nader's facility with newspaper publicity slowed about the same time as the FANS effort, as well. One prime example is with the *Washington Post*. Morton Mintz, who had worked closely with Nader in past years, was shuttled off to cover other news beats and he, along with other reporters in the Washington bureau, was not permitted to write stories about Nader. Administration of the paper had changed, and the *Post* had become pro-business.

Nader attributed this to his nonsociability and said, "I'm really sorry I didn't do more of that.... That was a mistake."[18]

Anti-Nader books also began showing up around this time. In 1975, journalist Ralph de Toledano published *Hit and Run: The Rise—and Fall?—of Ralph Nader*. On the dust jacket cover he wrote,

Nader's consumerism has little to do with the consumer, with improved products and services, or with the needs of the citizenry. It is an ideologically motivated effort to take control of industry from the producers and to turn it over to government and to the Naderites. This is statism, pure and simple— a kind of national socialism since Nader suffers from a suspicion of foreign countries bordering on xenophobia. It is this which converted and debased the legitimate concerns of the true consumers into a politically destructive force, which sowed distrust and suspicion of all the institutions of this country.... [19]

The following year, David Sanford, who authored *Hot War on the Consumer* and *Who Put the Con in Consumer?* with Nader, penned *Me & Ralph, Is Nader Unsafe for America?* He wrote,

I hope that this book will put the Nader myth in a new perspective. He is not a fit subject for hagiography but a man with human faults and motives that are no different and no less venal than those of other men. We sneer at politicians for their hungers and their lack of principle. Nader is as ravenous as a Nixon or a Kennedy, and the abstract principles he espouses he does not live by. Like the rest of us, he cuts corners.[20]

While facing the prospect of defeat, Nader did as any good general would and pulled his association with the Nader operations back. He stepped down as president of Public Citizen, and because he and Claybrook had patched things up, she was named Public Citizen's new president. Though he did still consult with the organization, he was no longer its administrator and that suited him. He preferred to be the stalking tiger on his own and promptly set himself in another direction. Though Nader was down, he was far from out.

NOTES

1. "Ford and Reagan Battle Down to Wire...Carter Addresses Nader Forum." *Facts On File World News Digest*, 14 August 1976. FACTS.com, http://www.2facts.com.

2. Frances Cerra, "Consumers Support Position of Carter," *New York Times*, 24 October 1976, p. 30.

3. Cerra, "Consumers Support Position of Carter," p. 30.

4. David Brian Robertson, ed., *Loss of Confidence: Politics and Policy in the 1970s*, vol. 10 (University Park: Pennsylvania State University Press, 1998), p. 70.

5. Quoted in Justin Martin, *Nader, Crusader, Spoiler, Icon* (New York: Perseus, 2002), p. 182.

6. Nixon participated in a cover-up of the activities of operatives, called the plumbers, who were arrested for an attempt to bug the offices of the Democratic National Committee in the Watergate Hotel in 1972.

7. Terrence R. Fehner and Jack M. Holl, *Department of Energy 1977–1994, A Summary History* (Oak Ridge, TN: Office of Scientific and Technical Information, 1994), p. 21.

8. Fehner and Holl, *Department of Energy 1977–1994, A Summary History*, p. 21.

9. Quoted in Herbert D Rosenbaum and Alexej Ugrinsky, *The Presidency and Domestic Policies of Jimmy Carter* (Westport, CT: Greenwood Press, 1994), p. 582.

10. Kenneth E. Morris, *Jimmy Carter, American Moralist* (Athens: University of Georgia Press, 1996), p. 256.

11. Quoted in Ernest Holsendolph, "Nader Calls on Ex-Colleague to Resign Safety Post," *New York Times*, 1 December 1977, p. 18.

12. Quoted in Holsendolph, "Nader Calls on Ex-Colleague to Resign Safety Post," p. 18.

13. Quoted in Holsendolph, "Nader Calls on Ex-Colleague to Resign Safety Post," p. 18.

14. Quoted in Holsendolph, "Nader Calls on Ex-Colleague to Resign Safety Post," p. 18.

15. Roger Skurski, ed. *New Directions in Economic Justice* (Notre Dame, IN: University of Notre Dame Press, 1983), p. 191.

16. Robert J. Buckley speaking to an audience at Fordham University, "Consumerism and the Economic Dope Habit, Making a Pygmy out of the Jolly Green Giant," *Vital Speeches of the Day*, 17 August 1977, pp. 145–50.

17. Quoted in Buckley "Consumerism and the Economic Dope Habit, Making a Pygmy out of the Jolly Green Giant," pp. 145–50.

18. Quoted in Martin, *Nader, Crusader, Spoiler, Icon*, p. 197.

19. Ralph de Toledano, *Hit & Run, the Rise—And Fall?—of Ralph Nader* (New Rochelle, NY: Arlington House, 1975), dust jacket.

20. David Sanford, *Me & Ralph, Is Nader Unsafe for America?* (Washington, D.C.: New Republic Book, 1976), p. xii.

Chapter 8

REBOUND

The end of the Carter era issued in a new Republican regime led by Ronald Reagan. To most liberals, this spelled disaster because of Reagan's interest in deregulation of industry and the lifting of legislative constraints on big business. Of course, to Ralph Nader, Reagan's policies were his undoing.

Nader's assumption that Congress was his sword to be wielded in the direction of big business had been broken. Congressional kowtowing to lobby groups frustrated him, and he found resistance where there was once admiration and cooperation. Senators had become inured to Nader's tactics and found some of them irritating and even egotistical. Certain senators and representatives were shunning Nader, and he found it impossible to gain any rapport with the Republican administration. In fact, the Republican administration would not even lend him an ear.

Reagan brought a touch of glamour to the presidency. As a former actor, he knew how to put on a great show. For the first time in history, the presidential inauguration was held on the west side of the Capitol building. Traditionally, presidents had been sworn in on the east portico. Yet, the west side provided a wonderful view of the Washington Monument across the grand expanse of the Mall. Reagan had come a long way in his life, from the time when he saved more than 30 lives in his years as a lifeguard at Lowell Park in Dixon, Illinois, to his days as a radio broadcaster, then actor, spokesman for General Electric, host of *Death Valley Days* on television, governor of California, and ultimately, president. Reagan had come up the hard way and had hard solutions to the country's ills.

Reagan's larger-than-life persona served well for rousing American spirits. Rising inflation, soaring unemployment, and American hostages taken by Iranian Muslim zealots had marked the Carter years as hard times. In a final blow, though Carter had orchestrated the release of the hostages, their liberation came at the precise moment Reagan was sworn into office—a sign of Iranian disdain for the Carter administration. After all that the United States had suffered during the past few years, Reagan's cumbersome onus was that of raising American morale through greater assertiveness, improvement of the economy, and a fall back to traditional American ideals.

In his inaugural address, Reagan said, "Well, this administration's objective will be a healthy, vigorous, growing economy that provides equal opportunity for all Americans, with no barriers born of bigotry or discrimination. Putting America back to work means putting all Americans back to work."[1] Reagan concentrated mainly on restoring a strong economy, creating a system labeled as Reaganomics. Biographer Edmund Morris wrote,

> There was no doubt, however, that Reagan and his economic aides had brought about the largest spending-control bill, and the largest tax reduction, in American history. Their budget was revolutionary in that it reversed—or, more properly, inversed—an economic theory dating back to the first days of the New Deal. Hallowed by Franklin Roosevelt, intellectualized by John Maynard Keynes, trumped by John Kenneth Galbraith, and codified by the social engineers of the Sixties and Seventies, the theory called for high, progressive tax rates, manipulative government spending, welfare-state "entitlements" centering around Social Security and Medicare/Medicaid, plus forcible downward redistribution of wealth and capital.[2]

Reagan's budget director, David Stockman, disagreed vehemently with the plan, understanding that the huge tax cuts and Social Security benefits Reagan planned would send the country into a downward spiral of deficit spending.

Reagan's economic policies were based in a theory known as the Laffer Curve, which suggests that as tax rates rise, government income rises; however, tax rates can only increase to a certain point before workers realize that so much of their income goes to the government that it pays them not to work as hard. At a 100 percent tax rate, no one would work, as all working income would go to the government. Reaganomics allowed for a lower tax rate, encouraging people to work harder because they were enabled to keep more of their income, thus providing more tax revenue for the federal government.

Nader saw Reagan's administration not only as an administration of questionable economics, but also as a heavy blow to consumerism. At Public Citizen, a mock wake was held to acknowledge the death of the consumer movement the day Reagan took office, and the Naderites' fears would soon come to fruition. Reagan set out his plans for deregulating industry almost immediately.

THE BUSINESS ROUNDTABLE

As a Republican, Reagan automatically leaned toward big business, and chief executive officers (CEOs) of major corporations had also become more adept at lobbying because of an organization formed in 1972—the Business Roundtable (BRT). The BRT was a merger of three different organizations that had been meeting informally to discuss public issues and policy. The March groups comprised CEOs from companies such as Alcoa and General Electric. The Construction Users Anti-Inflation Roundtable, with members from such companies as U.S. Steel, focused on keeping construction costs down. The Labor Law Study Committee had a membership of labor relations executives throughout the country. The new organization was founded with this purpose:

> The executives who created the Roundtable believed that the U.S. economy would be healthier, there would be less unwarranted intrusion by government into business affairs, and the interest of the public would be better served if there were more cooperation and less antagonism. It was decided that one way business could be a more constructive force and have more impact on government policymaking was to bring the Chief Executives directly into the picture. The Roundtable therefore was formed with two major goals:
>
> • To enable chief executives from different corporations to work together to analyze specific issues affecting the economy and business, and
> • To present government and the public with knowledgeable, timely information and with practical, positive suggestions for action.[3]

Nader and his followers saw this as an attempt by big business to present their own united front to Congress, which would be warmly received by the new administration and counteract the Naderites' position.

Reagan did not hesitate to implement deregulation, which began two days after he took office. First, he created the Task Force on Regulatory Relief, which was to be headed by Vice President George H.W. Bush. In his remarks to announce the new task force, Reagan said, "Government regulations impose an enormous burden on large and small businesses in America, discourage productivity, and contribute substantially to our current economic woes. To cut away the thicket of irrational and senseless regulations requires careful study, [and] close coordination between the agencies and bureaus in the Federal structure."[4]

To further enhance the ability of the task force to deal with its obligations of assessing existing regulations and overseeing the development of any new regulations, Reagan imposed Executive Order 12291 on February 17, 1981. The regulations to be supervised were those with

1. An annual effect on the economy of $100 million or more;
2. A major increase in costs or prices for consumers; individual industries; Federal, State, or local government agencies; or geographic regions; or
3. Significant adverse effects on competition, employment, investment, productivity, innovation, or on the ability of United States-based enterprises to compete with foreign-based enterprises in domestic or export markets.[5]

Along with Vice President Bush, the task force's members included other staunch Republicans, such as Treasury Secretary Donald Regan, Attorney General W.F. Smith, Commerce Secretary Malcolm Baldridge, Labor Secretary Raymond Donovan, OMB Director David Stockman, Council of Economic Advisors Chairman Murray Weidenbaum, and Assistant to President Reagan, Martin Anderson.

INSTANT DEFEATS

Soon, GM and the National Highway Traffic Safety Administration (NHTSA) gave the task force issues to consider by jointly criticizing regulations that caused the price of a new car to rise $400 per vehicle. After a cost-benefit analysis by the Office of Management and Budget (OMB), the task force proposed to eliminate or delay 34 environmental and safety regulations for cars and trucks because it was determined that these actions would save $1.4 billion in capital costs and $9.3 billion for consumers over the next five years. Some of the rules to be eased included eliminating stricter emission standards and allowing a one-year delay in mandatory passive restraints on automobiles, which included air bags or automatically fastening front-seat belts. Nader was furious, and when the NHTSA scrapped the air bag idea entirely in October, he threatened a lawsuit.

The Reagan administration also imposed deep budget cuts, affecting agencies such as the NHTSA and the Federal Trade Commission (FTC), which budgets dropped by 22 and 28 percent respectively. But when they started weakening the Occupational Health and Safety Administration (OSHA), Nader did not merely threaten, he took the matter to court. The case *Public Citizen Health Research Group v. Tyson* [796 F. 2d 1479 (D.C. Cir. 1986)] was filed when the OMB ordered OSHA to rescind a short-term exposure limit for workers using ethylene oxide, a sterilizing agent found to be carcinogenic for humans. Public Citizen also sued OSHA to enforce limits on other workplace hazards, such as the acceptable amount of grain dust that could accumulate on a silo floor and forcing pharmaceutical companies to replace the label on bottles of aspirin to warn parents of the dangers of Reye's syndrome in children with influenza or chicken pox. The battles were long and exhausting and it often took years before the courts made any decisions.

In a 1982 letter to Reagan, Nader lamented that the federal government was whittling away consumer protection. He accused Reagan of allying with corporations and disregarding safety for the people the government was there to represent. An assistant press secretary, Mark Weinberg, crafted a response saying that Reagan believed that federal regulation was unnecessary and expensive and that free enterprise, rather than a burgeoning bureaucracy, was much more important to the public's interest. With this, Nader saw that his options were not just limited when it came to Washington, but nil.

His epiphany was that he was targeting energy on the wrong focus. Rather than dealing with government bent upon destroying the foundations he had laid for consumer rights, he had decided to go back to the people. Returning to an old idea Campaign GM used, Nader had already begun to gather groups of citizens for greater clout in affecting change. He wrote, "Banding together as buyers can broaden and metabolize the community quest for economic justice and liberate both political and economic thinkers from their invisible chains of thought."[6]

RALLYING THE MASSES

Nader's army of individual consumer organizations first took on the task of battling high utility bills, and he called them Residential Utility

Consumer Action Groups (RUCAGs). The first was organized in Wisconsin in 1979. The premise was to have each RUCAG as an independent, nonprofit organization that would fight for state legislation to force utility companies to include invitations to all of their customers to join RUCAGs, stuffed right into their regular monthly utility bills. When interested consumers signed up, a nominal fee (usually less than one dollar) would be charged, along with their monthly utility bill balance. As with Public Interest Research Groups (PIRGs), the RUCAG money was used to hire attorneys and accountants who could fight consumers' battles for them. Not only did the utilities have to pay for the postage for the membership drive, but to abet the very organization that would be fighting against them. Nader also hired full-time organizers to go around the country promoting the idea, and by the early 1980s, groups were active in Wisconsin, San Diego, and Oregon, though the dissonant-sounding acronym RUCAG was soon changed to the more melodious-sounding CUB (Consumer Utility Board).

In 1986, CUBs had a significant setback when the U.S. Supreme Court ruled, in a split decision, that forcing companies to stuff the CUB flyers into utility bills violated the utilities' "negative free speech rights" (the right not to speak), guaranteed by the first amendment. Since then, CUBs have resorted to less-direct means of attracting members.

CUBs still exist in four states—Illinois, Wisconsin, Oregon, and California, and their fight is no longer limited to the price of home heating oil. In addition to watching those prices, CUBs fight for fair cable TV rates; fair electric, gas, and water rates; and fair telephone usage prices. These coalitions have been very successful. In the Illinois CUB alone, the 170,000 members have saved more than $4 billion.

In 1982, Nader founded Essential Information to encourage citizenship in America and to promote issues not covered by the national media. The organization publishes a monthly magazine, books, and reports and sponsors an investigative journalism conference, along with providing grants for writers who want to pursue investigations. About two years earlier, Nader had organized the Corporate Accountability Research Group (CARG), which continues to publish the *Multinational Monitor*, which runs monthly exposés regarding international corporations.

In 1985, Nader also had a hand in forming the Foundation for Taxpayer and Consumer Rights (FTCR), another tax exempt, nonprofit organization. From its inception, the FTCR has been led by consumer activist and attorney Harvey Rosenfield and employs a team of public interest lawyers, strategists, teachers, activists, and policy experts that delve into many areas, with the aim of protecting the interests of American tax-

payers. Some projects include the protection of personal privacy and pa-
tients' rights, grassroots organizing and training, and preserving the voters' will.

During this grassroots push, Nader also went on the offensive regarding
public access to the airwaves. In 1987, he wrote in the *Chicago Tribune*,
"The gross inequality of electronic access through the working of exclusive license authorities forces the public to rely on a few corporations' per-
ceptions of society, politics, the arts, and the public itself. A democracy
does not thrive when information sources, values, and access remain so
limited."[7] He argued that the public legally owned the airwaves and that
viewers had the right to decide their own programming, but that the Federal Communications Commission (FCC) took available airwaves and
simply divided them among the networks.

This led Nader to found Citizen's Television in Buffalo, New York. He
acquired the license, as one of 800 in an FCC lottery for low-power television (LPTV). With the station's ownership listed as "Citizens Television
System, Inc.," Nader took over Channel 58 with call letters WFHW-LP
and ran it on a meager budget of about $50,000 a year. Advertisements
sold for $10 a spot to local businesses that could not afford the cost of net-
work time. The station provided broadcasts of community government
along with entertainment, including programs with ethnic dancing and
restaurant reviews. With its scant budget and crew of young broadcast
hopefuls, the station functioned much like the Nader's Raiders of television.

Also around this time, Nader became interested in the cost of heating
oil. Distillate fuel, including diesel fuel and heating oil, cost $5.35 per mil-
lion BTUs in 1979,[8] but rose sharply to its highest cost up to that time—
$9.19 per million BTU in 1981. Alarmed by such high prices, Nader
formed Buyers Up in 1983, a consortium of home heating oil customers in
the Washington, D.C., area, a group able to wield influence to make heating oil companies discount their product. In its first year, Buyers Up en-
rolled 850 households, but the organization, which is operated by Public
Citizen, has grown to a membership of more than 4,000 members in 2004
and continues to negotiate with home heating oil companies.

ATTRACTING AN AUDIENCE

As with all the groups Nader founded or had an interest in organizing,
once his role had been played, he left the group to continue with little or
no input from him again. Throughout this time, Nader also continued to
make rounds of speaking engagements throughout the country. American

Program Bureau (APB) continues to represent Nader and touts him as one of *Time* magazine's "100 Most Influential Americans of the 20th century." To illustrate his message, APB provides the following on its Web site: "To go through life as a non-citizen would be to feel that there's nothing you can do, that nobody's listening, that you don't matter. But to be a citizen is to enjoy the deep satisfaction of seeing the prevention of pain, misery and injustice."[9]

Nader continues a rigorous speaking schedule and said that he makes different types of speeches all over the country: "Some of them are right here in Washington, too—with high school students. I do the Presidential Classroom gathering several times a year and then, there are ones around the country. I would say [I make] about a hundred speeches a year."[10] Other of his current speech topics for the American Program Bureau include the following: "Democracy, Big Business and the American Duopoly"; "While You Were Watching 'Big Brother,' 'Big Brother' Was Watching You: What Students Should Know, What Students Can Do"; and "The Corporatization of America."

In the mid-1980s, Nader's opening line was, "How many of you are hungry to become fighters for justice in America?"[11] He most enjoyed speaking to law students and particularly enjoyed prodding those at Harvard Law School, his alma mater. He delivered a speech there on June 11, 1985, entitled, "Harvard Lawyers: Nabobs of Narcissism Wallowing in Complacency?"[12] Regardless of his irreverence, or maybe because of it, students packed auditoriums to hear him. Even corporations began to hire him to speak to their employees about customer satisfaction.

In April 1986, Nader published *The Big Boys,* co-authored with William Taylor and Andrew Moore. In it, nine corporate leaders were interviewed, including David Roderick of U.S. Steel, Paul Oreffice of Dow Chemical, and William Norris of Control Data. The book examined their personalities and management styles in view of how they influenced the industries in which they functioned. In an editorial, avowed liberal Robert Lekachman of *The Nation* wrote, "Two who have kept their faith, sanity and temper have just reminded us again that perseverance pays, that intelligence can vanquish organized greed and that good guys sometimes win" (referring to Nader and to Michael Pertschuk, former FTC chairman under Jimmy Carter and then Ronald Reagan, who had also written a book at the same time, entitled *Giantkillers,* showing that public interest lobbyists could be successful against corporations).

Though *The Big Boys* was an interesting examination of power and the men who wield it, Nader, Taylor, and Andrews also pointed out the leaders' inability to address human needs outside the corporation. Yet, the book got little attention and in other publications, bad reviews.

At this juncture, Nader still seemed to be as popular with the citizenry of America as he was unpopular with the media and Congress. However, his lack of governmental support and bad or no publicity did not stop his crusade. He continued to argue the consumer, civics issues plaguing the country for the good of the American people. In 1986, however, events that were devastating to him personally brought him to a temporary halt.

A TIME TO HEAL

The first blow to Nader came about when he developed Bell's palsy, a condition that causes the muscles of the face to become weak or paralyzed. The illness is named for Sir Charles Bell, who studied the facial nerves and muscles in the nineteenth century. Bell's palsy is considered a rare disease in that it strikes only one in 5,000, but it affects 40,000 Americans each year.

Bell's palsy can strike anyone of any age, though the greatest number of sufferers are pregnant women, diabetics, and those suffering a cold, influenza, or other upper respiratory illnesses. The disease affects the seventh cranial nerve, and herpes simplex 1, the virus, which also causes cold sores to the mouth, is a possible antagonist, as are autoimmune disorders or circulatory problems. Nader asserted that his palsy was caused by breathing recirculated air inside an airplane.

With Bell's palsy, unilateral paralysis of the face may be accompanied by the inability to close one eye or other symptoms, such as drooling, pain, hypersensitivity to sound on the stricken side, and the inability to taste. Symptoms arise suddenly. Often people notice the problem upon waking; however, neck pain or pain behind the ear are sometimes warning signals and onset occurs within hours.

The left side of Nader's face was paralyzed. His left eye could not blink and constantly dripped with tears. The full effects of the disease subsided, though the course of normal healing and recovery was extended in Nader's case. Usual recovery time is about two weeks, but Nader continued to have difficulty with the muscles on the affected side of his face and his eyelid drooped for months. To mask these effects, Nader wore sunglasses and kidded that no one could then accuse him of talking out of both sides of his mouth.

Although the prognosis for Bell's palsy is a gradual full recovery, for some it never goes away. "There are certain residual manifestations,"

Nader said, "but it's pretty tolerable. The distortion has gone away."[13] People seeing Nader in public, unless they were aware that he once had the disease, would say that his face looks normal. Yet, there are still slight indications that the healing process was never complete if one studies the left side of Nader's face. There is a 10 to 20 percent likelihood of recurrence, with the average time span between attacks at 10 years.

Bell's Palsy was not the only adversity Nader would encounter that year. In August, Nader lost his brother Shafeek to prostate cancer. Shafeek's death was deeply devastating for Nader, as it was for the entire family. Nader had been close to his older brother, who had recommended reading material for him as a young boy and lit the spark that ignited Nader's lifelong interest in baseball.

A BROTHER'S DREAMS

Shafeek Nader had also espoused the philosophies of his father when it came to activism and citizenship. When Nader went to Washington to fight corporations, Shafeek went back to Winsted, after graduating from the University of Toronto, to help with the restaurant and the community. In 1959, when the old Gilbert school was moved to a new building, the old school remained vacant. Shafeek saw it as an ideal center for a community college. As with many of the Naders' ideas, this notion was viewed with skepticism. The people of Winsted did not see the need for a community college in such a small town. Yet, Shafeek persisted and saw the new community college—Northwestern Connecticut Community College—established, making Winsted the smallest American town to have a community college of its own.

That was not the extent of Shafeek's dreams for the town. He also proposed that Winsted, a landlocked village, should have its own fishing boat on the Atlantic Ocean, which could troll for fish and make money for the town. Harold Fleming, a retired anthropologist and lifelong resident of Winsted once said, "Winsted was never a town with much fighting spirit. It's a bedroom community now, but when Nader was growing up, it was a factory town run by the factories: Union busting was widespread, pollution was rampant, few people went to college, or fought for their rights. People just murmured."[14] Believing that most important decisions were made at the grassroots level, Shafeek fought hard for the causes he believed in, just as Nader fought for them in Washington, D.C.

Shafeek also spent time in Washington, as did all the Nader siblings at one time or another. In 1971, he purchased a home in Kalorama, one of the most prestigious neighborhoods in Washington, D.C., with quick access to the White House, the Capitol, and Dulles International Airport. All the Naders spent time there, and so although Ralph worked in one state and Shafeek in another, their relationship continued to be strong into adulthood.

Yet, reporters used the house on Bancroft Place to debunk the notion that the currently successful Nader continued to live in the boarding-house on 19th St. NW, though that is the image Nader continued to portray. For him to live in an expensive house, worth about $100,000 at the time (about $1.5 million today) would destroy his image as the icon of frugality and set people to wondering why he lived well when paying his workers so little. Nader told *Washington Post* columnist Maxine Cheshire that Shafeek had purchased the property because he wanted to live full-time in Washington and become an educational consultant. Cheshire wrote, "The house sold with a down payment of $20,000 and mortgage payments of $370 per month. That would not fit Ralph Nader's carefully cultivated austerity image. Since Shafeek's death, Claire Nader has owned the property. When asked if he lived as frugally as he did in the past, Nader said, "Yes, adjusted for inflation,"[15] and did not elaborate.

Biographer Robert F. Buckhorn wrote, "Nader is testy about his private income. Like his rooming house, his love life, and his family, he feels strongly that this is not a matter of public concern."[16] Although this would remain true for years, events would make Nader's finances public. Still, before 2000, Nader's personal life and finances remained confidential. "Privacy is important to me. I have only a little left, and I am not letting go of it."[17]

Perhaps Nader's health was a matter of privacy to him, as well. After his bout with Bell's palsy and the death of his brother, he went back to Winsted, where he remained for three months, out of the spotlight and away from his work. Knowing his desire to remain a private individual while directly in the public eye, his hiatus from the public arena seemed right during his time of personal distress. He was gearing up for another personal agenda, one that would make him the darling of one sector, while increasing the ire of another.

NOTES

1. Ronald Reagan, "First Inaugural Address of Ronald Reagan," *The Avalon Project at Yale Law School*, 3 December 2003, http://www.yale.edu/lawweb/avalon/president/inaug/reagan1.htm.

2. Edmund Morris, *Dutch, a Memoir of Ronald Reagan* (New York: Random House, 1999), p. 446.

3. "What the Roundtable Is, Why It Was Founded, How It Works," *The Business Roundtable*, 2001, http://www.businessroundtable.org/about.cfm/history.

4. Ronald Reagan, "Remarks Announcing the Establishment of the Presidential Task Force on Regulatory Relief," *Official Web Site of the Ronald Reagan Presidential Library*, 22 January 1981, http://www.reagan.utexas.edu/resource/speeches/1981/12281c.htm.

5. Ronald Reagan, Executive Order, EO12291, 17 February 1981.

6. Ralph Nader, "The Consumer Movement Looks Ahead," (New York: Harper & Row, 1984), reprinted in *The Ralph Nader Reader*, (New York: Seven Stories Press, 2000), p. 228.

7. Ralph Nader, "Let's Put the Audience on the Air," *Chicago Tribune*, 27 May 1987, reprinted in Ralph Nader, *The Ralph Nader Reader* (New York: Seven Stories Press, 2000), p. 437.

8. British Thermal Units (BTU). The temperature equivalent to 251.996 Calories, 778.26 foot pounds, or nearly 1/3 watt hours.

9. "Ralph Nader," *American Program Bureau*, http://www.apbspeakers.com/main/ info.asp?id=0232.

10. Ralph Nader, interview with the author, 15 August 2003.

11. Quoted in Justin Martin, *Nader, Crusader, Spoiler, Icon* (New York: Perseus, 2002), p. 213.

12. Quoted in Martin, *Nader, Crusader, Spoiler, Icon*, p. 213.

13. Nader, interview with the author, 15 August 2003.

14. Quoted in Joanna Weiss, "A Totem to Torts, Some See Museum Plan as Only a Nader Tribute," *Boston Globe*, 17 October 2000.

15. Nader, interview with the author, 15 August 2003.

16. Robert F. Buckhorn, *Nader the People's Lawyer* (Englewood Cliffs, NJ: Prentice-Hall, 1972), p. 152.

17. Buckhorn, *Nader the People's Lawyer*, p. 152.

Chapter 9

BACK IN ACTION

When Ralph Nader went into seclusion, he had reached a low point in his life. Those in power saw him as an irritant and people were tired of fighting for causes and spending more money for legislation that proved listless in its final form. Though the benefits of safety or fairness were doubtlessly beneficial, victories came with a price. People paid more for new cars with safety features, such as seat belts, padded dashboards, and soon to be included, front air bags in every vehicle. Consumers saw their paychecks shrinking as they were under mandatory deductions to support the Occupational Health and Safety Administration (OSHA). Even Nader's staunchest supporters had begun to wonder if crusades were worth the price. Joan Claybrook said, "Ralph just withdrew for three months after [Shafeek] died."[1]

Nader may have been down, but he was certainly not out. He continued to be informed and followed issues that interested him, though they were on the grassroots level, and did not garner public attention. During this time, he had also begun to follow efforts to limit consumers' rights to sue for damages, via no-fault insurance. The idea infuriated him. "You can never be made whole for pain and suffering," he said.[2] This interest eventually developed into his being drafted to support Proposition 103 (Prop 103) in California, which demanded a rollback in insurance premiums of 20 percent for autos, homes, businesses, and all other property casualty premiums. It also stipulated strict controls for insurance companies, which were seen as gouging Californians for premiums that had increased 22 percent between 1985 and 1987 for automobiles alone, and the public was every bit as outraged as Nader.

For many years, consumers had been ignored in the California state legislature. The Association of California Insurance Companies (ACIC) had dumped huge sums into political contributions, thus preventing any rate reforms. Instead, the ACIC encouraged legislators to support bills meant to reduce or limit legal fees and damage awards to victims. Of course, trial lawyers struck back by encouraging rate reductions, rather than limitations to their fees or plaintiff's awards. This tug-of-war, with consumers placed squarely atop the center knot, had become not only tiresome, but also expensive. Californians were fed up and when Nader stepped into the picture, the general feeling was one of relief. Their St. George had arrived.

Yet, more than rates and awards were at issue. Other provisions of Prop 103 involved requiring insurance companies to place liability on the drivers' safety records, rather than on their place of residence. It mandated a good driver discount of 20 percent. Moreover, contrary to then-current practice, it stipulated that the state insurance commissioner be elected rather than appointed.

The skirmish over this proposed change became fierce and three sides battled for control. Pollsters advised the insurance industry that no matter how much money they threw into the campaign to defeat Prop 103 it would pass. Thus, in answer to the proposed regulations in Prop 103, insurance companies initially came back with measures of their own, which were the following:

Prop 101: limited payments for pain and suffering and countering of every provision in Prop 103

Prop 104: required a no-fault insurance system in California, via which the parties involved in an accident are covered by their own insurance companies, regardless of blame; also required that injuries sustained in auto accidents should first be covered by a victim's own health insurance before being eligible for coverage under auto policies, which, if approved, would logically drive up the cost of health insurance

These provisos carried a clever strategy. Included within the legalese of Prop 104, especially, were provisions that directly conflicted with Prop 103. Insurance companies knew that the California Constitution would prevail. Article II, section 10(b) says that in the event that both Propositions 103 and 104 passed, the proposition with the largest number of votes would win. With their huge advertising budget, the ACIC hoped to accumulate more votes than Prop 103, which would invalidate Prop 103, even if it were accepted by a majority of the people.

TRAIL LAWYERS REACT

When the insurance industry's answers to Prop 103 came out, it naturally raised the ire of trial lawyers, who take personal injury and consumer advocacy cases. Once derided as "ambulance chasers," these litigators became a well-accepted arm of the legal profession when Nader began fighting corporations and consumer causes in court. He single-handedly raised the practice of tort law to new heights.[3]

The California Trial Lawyers Association (CTLA) was infuriated by the insurance companies' intent to limit their contingency fees, to reduce the amount of litigation via no-fault insurance, and to limit awards to plaintiffs to keep their profits up, while taking money from both victims and their lawyers. In answer, the CTLA filed Proposition 100, which contained language to prohibit any restrictions on attorney's fees and to cancel the insurance industry's propositions should it get more votes than the ACIC proposals.

That was not the end of propositioning. The insurance industry came back with Proposition 106 to place higher limitations on the percentage lawyers could charge to take cases on a contingency basis,[4] by placing a 25 percent cap for the first $50,000 of any damage claim award, 15 percent on the next $50,000, and 10 percent on any portion over $100,000. The ACIC and the CTLA had basically targeted each other, figuring Proposition 103 would fail because of lack of funding and the needed support to get the initiative on the ballot.

Enough signatures were attained to get all five propositions on the November 1988 ballot, which gave the ACIC reason to worry. The fact that the public wanted lower rates was clear. Thus, the insurance companies came up with a new strategy to attack the constitutionality of Prop 103 in court. However, both a lower court and the State Supreme Court on appeal dismissed the case.

CALLING IN THE BIG GUNS

Harvey Rosenfield, president of the Foundation for Taxpayer and Consumer Rights (FTCR) and a leader in adopting Prop 103 (formally known as "The Insurance Rate Reduction and Reform Act of 1988), had also been a Nader's Raider. He knew that to compete with the ACIC's advertising budget, the consumer groups needed money and some strong muscle. So, he enlisted the help of Nader, who said, "[The California insurance crisis is] the greatest commercial hoax that I have ever observed in the United States, both in terms of its size—tens of billions of dollars—and in terms of its manufactured figures and phony anecdotes...For ten months now, I have challenged the insurance industry to tell us how much they are paying out in verdicts and settlements from year to year and break it down by commercial line...And they haven't done it."[5]

Nader and Rosenfield started a campaign organization, which Nader named Voter's Revolt to Cut Insurance Rates or succinctly, Voter's Revolt. Rosenfield then hired professional vote gatherers and spent $2.9 million, the bulk of which paid for solicitations to consumers to send $10 each. The media jumped into the fray and heavily advertised the side of Voters' Revolt, thus providing free advertising and education for the initiative.

The day before the election, public support for Prop 103 had risen to 74 percent. Yet, with all sides battling and the ACIC and the CTLA advertising heavily, the public became confused, and did not understand the whole matter between the rivaling factions. The only thing they were sure of was Prop 103. It passed easily on November 8, 1988.

Not everyone, even without ties to the insurance or legal industries, was pleased. Some called the victory too controlling, as it called for drastic rate reduction. "The [Naderites] do not care how or whether the industry will survive—they simply want to place it under the domination of the state," wrote Peter Schwartz, Chief Executive Officer of the Ayn Rand Institute. "A business cannot exist if forced to live on income of years past while having to meet the costs of today."[6]

In truth, Prop 103 threw the insurance industry into chaos. Companies paid back $1.2 billion in excessive premiums charged to customers in the 1980s, and the average liability premium dropped 22 percent between 1989 and 2001, while the national average rose more than 30 percent.

Yet, the insurance industry shrank from attacking Nader publicly. He was much too popular. People loved him for what he had done. Michael Kinsey, former Nader Raider, co-host of CNN's *Crossfire*, then editor of *The New Republic (TNR)* magazine wrote, "In all statistical probability, at least several dozen of you who are reading this issue of *TNR* would be dead today if Nader hadn't single-handedly invented the issue of auto safety."[7] Though advocates such as Senator Abraham A. Ribicoff and Harold A. Katz, who wrote the auto safety article to ignite Nadar's interest back in 1956, had been involved in the topic long before Nader entered the picture, he was perceived as the father of this issue because of the incredible publicity generated by the General Motors (GM) scandal.

RESURRECTION

In 1989, Nader took on another task, more humanitarian in nature than his usual consumer advocacy, though the two fields here are closely related. He went back to his undergraduate alma mater, Princeton, and suggested that his graduating class should be more effective in combating social ills plaguing the country. This idea developed into Princeton Project 55 (PP55), an independent nonprofit organization, which supports organizations, students, and young alumni of Princeton, working in the public interest. In 1997, Nader and Dr. Gordon Douglas, former president of Merck pharmaceuticals' Vaccine Division and both members of the Princeton class of 1955, tackled the issue of tuberculosis, which has historically been the world's biggest killer. Efforts to stem the disease continue today. These humanitarian efforts continued to increase Nader's stature and his place in the hearts of a large segment of the American population.

Another project in 1989 enhanced Nader's appeal when he turned his direction back to a broader issue that also involved a former issue for him—the national ownership of public airwaves. However, this time his fight not only included the airwaves, but all publicly owned domains, what Nader calls "taxpayer assets." These assets also include national forests, waterways, coastal lands, and minerals, all owned by the American public, but often used and abused to suit corporate interests. Robert C. Fellmeth began exploring this territory in his 1971 book, *Politics of Land*, which described such abuses in California. Another Nader-sponsored book, *Lost Frontier: The Marketing of Alaska*, written by Peter Gruenstein and John Hanrahan, showed how big companies were abusing that state, as well. A third book, *Public Domain, Private Dominion: A History of Public Mineral Policy in America*, written by Carl J. Mayer and George A. Riley, documented how the entire country's assets were being exploited in the same ways.

To create an advocacy group capable of dealing with this travesty, Nader founded the Taxpayer Assets Project in 1989. Director James P. Love organized a staff to look into areas where taxpayer assets were mismanaged and where they could be used to better advantage for the American public. This included fighting the federal government on its penchant for giving away intellectual property that was funded by American taxpayers, in the form of research and development or of information, gathered and given to "information vendors," who then profit by selling it to back to consumers and libraries.

TIME AS MONEY

Nader was involved in several more projects in 1989. He told Claybrook, "Things are popping again."[8] And Thomas A. Stewart, in *Fortune* magazine, quoted an anonymous insurance executive as saying, "We've resurrected Ralph Nader. It's like Lazarus."[9] Indeed, Nader's strong comeback at the end of 1988 and the following year sparked many new ideas. Another included in those thoughts was the concept of "Time Dollars." Although the idea originally came from Professor Edgar Cahn, devised while he was in the hospital recovering from a heart attack, Essential Information, founded by Nader in 1982, and the Center for Science in the Public Interest (CSPI), founded by Michael F. Jacobson in 1971, were major proponents of the idea. In expressing his idea, Cahn said, "The real wealth of a society is not money. It is the time of its citizens. Why couldn't we create a new kind of money to pay people—money not controlled by the government or the politicians and used to pay people to meet the needs of society?"[10] In Cahn's system, people work for credits to be exchanged when they needed work to be done for them or their family, friends, or even donate their credits to charity. To promote this idea, Essential Information gave Cahn vital financial support, as did other foundations. Nader wrote a primer on the topic and appeared on *The Donahue Show*, hosted by Phil Donahue to show his solidarity with the idea. On an *Inside Edition* segment, he said, "I have rarely seen an idea that has a higher predictability of sweeping the country."[11] Several time-dollar organizations sprang up around the country, and the idea extended overseas to European countries, such as the United Kingdom, and to Asian countries, such as Japan.

Nader saw time dollars as a way to protect the public's interest, just as he became concerned about insurance costs in California, which set the stage for other states to sit up and take notice. This public asset protection at the end of the 1980s made Nader the hero to many again; yet, at the beginning of the 1990s, Nader's sterling image tarnished somewhat. He was perceived as both saint and sinner, as media painted him as a friend to the trial lawyers when he spoke out vociferously against any tort reform legislation that would limit legal fees and the amounts awarded to victims in personal injury cases. Tort law covers civil wrongs that are not covered by contracts. For instance, Nader's case against GM for trying to demean his character was a case in tort law. Nader said, "Tort law is a major foundation of personal freedom and safety in America."[12]

Nader was not in the battle to support tort lawyers, as the media chastised, but carrying out what he felt was his moral obligation to consumers. It continues to be important to him that victims be allowed to recover damages, not only for physical harm, but for pain and suffering, such as a woman suffering the effects of faulty silicone breast implants or a child who loses sight because of a dangerous toy. Nader vehemently believes that those involved in such situations should be able to find some measure of recompense in awards achieved through the tort system of law. "Because Ralph is self-sustaining," said ex-aide Gary Sellers, "he is responsible only to his own conscience. The others aren't—they're in the middle of a web of interests, and they have to protect present income or future sources."[13] Therefore, Nader is against tort law reform because the present system protects consumers. The fact that lawyers are making the practice of law a business, rather than a profession, is a side issue.

TORT LAW: GOOD OR JUST EXPENSIVE?

Nader could be considered the poster boy for tort law because his causes and many of his organizations' causes focus on civil wrongdoing. The upside of these actions is safer cars, cleaner air and water, and cheaper utilities. The downside is that tort litigation purportedly cost taxpayers more than $233 billion in 2002 and rose by 13.3 percent from the year before, according to Tillinghast-Towers Perrin, which provides risk management services for the financial services industry.[14] Tillinghast's figures are considered the standard for government and industry. According to the company's study, the rate of growth in these costs was 10.3 percent higher than the gross domestic product (GDP) in 2002 and accounted for 2.23 percent of that figure, costing every person in America—man, woman, and child—$809 in that year.

Tillinghast projects medical malpractice as one of the largest growing segments in tort litigation, which costs have risen an average of 11.9 percent per year, amounting to $85 per person in 2002. Other causes for the rise in tort actions are claims stemming from exposure to asbestos, large monetary awards, higher numbers of shareholder lawsuits against boards of directors, and higher medical costs, which were driven upward by the size of awards made in personal injury cases.

The projected increase in tort litigation is 6 to 11 percent per year, with the 2005 costs projected at $1,003 per person. Many see these increases as a drain on the American economy, and perhaps rightly so, as the costs are nearly triple those of President George W. Bush's tax cuts of 2001 and 2003 combined.[15] Tort lawyers have long been perceived as promoting sometimes-frivolous court actions to line their own pockets. A New York think tank, Manhattan Institute for Policy Research, wrote in a 2003 report, " More and more, the [legal] industry resembles a racket designed to do little more than advance the incomes and interests of members—everyone else be damned."[16]

But there is another side to this issue. Americans for Insurance Reform (AIR), a national coalition of public interest groups that lobbies for insurance reform to curb rising rates, says that the Tillinghast report is wrong. AIR says that Tillinghast derives its figure using total liability insurance premiums reported by A.M. Best, an insurance reporting firm. AIR also stated that other costs such as auto insurance claims for minor accidents or no-fault medical payments, in which no lawyers take part, were included in Tillinghast's total figure. AIR criticizes Tillinghast for not considering jury verdicts, settlements, lawyers' fees, or actual costs of litigation, and holds that if Tillinghast had considered these figures, the cost would be lower by at least 50 percent. AIR also reports, "Tillinghast does not measure the countervailing costs saved by the tort system; nor does it place any value on the rights granted to all Americans by the tort system itself."[17]

ADVOCATING PUBLIC JUSTICE

Nader's personal interest in tort law is obvious. After his relationship with Roscoe Pound, he came to uphold that part of the legal system that deals with righting wrongs. In 1992, Nader urged a group of lawyers to form Trial Lawyers for Public Justice (TLPJ), a national, nonprofit, public interest law firm with the intent of using the skills of good lawyers to engender a better society. The TLPJ mission statement reads: "TLPJ fights for justice through precedent-setting and socially significant individual and class action litigation designed to enhance consumer and victims' rights, environmental protection and safety, civil rights and civil liberties, workers' rights, America's civil justice system, and the protection of the poor and powerless."[18]

Undoubtedly, the frivolity of lawsuits has proliferated over the past few decades. Lawsuits, such as the following, cost American taxpayers court time, whether they ultimately come to trial or not:

- Class-action suits, where there are an unspecified number of plaintiffs, blaming fast food chain restaurants for making people obese.

- An award of $2.2 million dollars from a suit brought by a convenience store worker because she injured her back opening a jar of pickles.

- Smokers with smoking-related illnesses who sue tobacco companies, when they burned and inhaled the product, while knowing that cigarettes are carcinogenic.

Many American see the tort system as having gotten out of hand. Few doubt that the American public has benefited from laws forcing car companies to install seat belts and air bags in every new vehicle, but should consumers really be able to file a lawsuit for not using their own common sense? Some wonder if hungry lawyers fuel people's greed.

The increased number of these well-publicized cases caused the shadow over trial lawyers to fall again, and within it was Nader. "We are what supports Nader," said attorney Frederic Levin of Florida. "We contribute to him and he fundraises through us."[19] Nader is seen as "one of them," and for that reason, trial lawyers hold him in high esteem. Nader's cause is their cause, regardless of divergent interests in tort law.

This battle over federal regulation of the tort system is still not resolved. Controversial with trial lawyers and some consumer advocates, tort law generally falls into the domain of each state. United States legislators do not readily enact laws that will impinge on states' rights, and so the issue is provocative, and quite complicated.

Scrutinizing taxpayer assets was a project directed toward government, rather than business. And in 1991, Nader became interested in the efforts of the legal system and the insurance companies to change how personal injury and corporate wrongdoings were handled in court.

PROFOUND LOSS AND FITTING TRIBUTE

When the issue of tort reform had begun to simmer in the early 1990s, Nader suffered another loss. Nathra died at age 99, just two months short of his 100th birthday, on July 7, 1991. Shortly thereafter, the Center for the Study of Responsive Law published a book entitled *It Happened in the Kitchen: Recipes for Food and Thought* by Rose B. Nader and Nathra Nader. In large part, it consisted of Rose Nader's own recipes, with generous smatterings of her wisdom on raising a family to accompany them. The last part of the book is a chapter of Nathra's maxims, which is introduced by the children, who also wrote short passages about the quotes to give Nathra's remarks context. One of his inimitable ideas was "There should be a dictionary of hypocrisy and hypocrites that comes out every year. That way, as each yearly edition gets thicker, we can better know what's happening to our society."[20] The children's caption follows: "Said during conversation about government euphemisms... [Here is] one that set off his absurdity bell: a 'unidirectional impact generator' to describe simple $10 claw hammers which a military contractor sold to the Pentagon for $450 each."[21] The book showed Nathra's spirit, along with Rose's good fresh food recipes and her recipes for life, and it is a fitting tribute to both Nader parents.

Though his father's death was certainly a personal tragedy, Nader had greater optimism for the future and was involved in many projects before and during this time—the Small Claims Study Group, in 1983, with the aim of helping citizens fight their own eligible legal battles in small claims courts; the founding, with Sidney Wolfe, of the Health Research Group, which tackled many issues including the ban on red dye no. 2, a food coloring that was nutritionally nil and carcinogenic, in 1971; and through the efforts of Nader and others, the Whistleblower Protection Act of 1989 finally became reality that spring when signed into law by President George H. W. Bush.

Nader's critics began to say that he had his fingers in too many pies at the same time. Yet, this complete involvement and his pattern of founding groups and then allowing the directors and officers to take over and run with the programs is his personal measure of success. He sees more corporations and government agencies under public scrutiny and more people involved in the process of citizenship, which is his ultimate goal. Claire Nader said, "The real measure of Ralph's success will be how many oak trees are planted."[22]

DESERT STORM/POLITICAL STORM

Nader continued to push various causes throughout 1990, but at the beginning of 1991, the country was anticipating a war. The Iraqi government had decided to annex Kuwait, an independent monarchy that had once been part of the Ottoman Empire, wherein it was given the status of principality, meaning it would have autonomy but still remain part of the empire. During World War I, the Ottomans, with the help of Germany, tried to take over domestic control of Kuwait again; however, Kuwait sought the protection of the British Empire, and the Ottomans were repelled. The British-Kuwaiti arrangement held until June 19, 1961, when British protection ended and Kuwait joined the Arab League, against Iraqi protests. However, in October 1963, Iraq formally gave up its claim on Kuwait.

Decades before then, oil had been discovered in Kuwait, and Gulf Oil, a British and U.S. company, was there to drill it, making Kuwait a tiny country with clout. Yet, internal political struggles in the late 1980s and a huge debt to Kuwait, stemming from the Iran-Iraq war of the 1980s, led Iraq to look at Kuwait with predatory and self-preserving intentions once again. Iraqis had hoped to pay the war debt back by increasing oil production in their own country, but Kuwait had increased production and lowered costs, hoping to gain leverage in Iraq-Kuwait border disputes, wherein the Iraqis had accused the Kuwaitis of drilling for oil and setting up military outposts on Iraqi soil. The Iraqis complained that they had buffered attacks for both Saudi Arabia and Kuwait against Iran on a continuing basis and should thereby be forgiven their debts.

Negotiations between Kuwait and Iraq failed, and on August 2, 1990, Iraq sent 100,000 troops across the Kuwaiti border to take control. Under the rule of Saddam Hussein, a period of severe oppression against the Kuwaiti people began and on August 8, Iraq formally announced Kuwait's annexation. The Arab League and the United Nations quickly denounced these claims and the Iraqi action, and the Iraqis were warned to withdraw, to no avail. On November 29, 1990, the Iraqis were given an ultimatum to leave Kuwait by January 15, 1991. On January 16, when Iraq did not comply, a coalition of 28 countries attacked Iraq to force Iraq out of Kuwait. In only six weeks, Kuwait was once again a sovereign nation.

About mid-1991, a presidential election was upcoming, and as the year progressed, hopefuls came from every part of the country, bearing diverse credentials and political views. Included in the run that spring, leading up to the primaries in February were Governor Bill Clinton (D-AR), incumbent President George H. W. Bush (R-TX), and Ross Perot, a Texas businessman running for the newly formed "Reform" party—the popular candidates in the 1992 election—but also Paul Tsongas (D-MA), columnist Pat Buchanan (R), and even Nader's old boss, Senator Daniel P. Moynihan, among a broad field of others. What no one knew, including Nader, was that he was about to reconsider his involvement in politics.

NOTES

1. Quoted in Thomas A. Stewart, "The resurrection of Ralph Nader," *Fortune*, 22 May 1999, pp. 106–10.

2. Quoted in Stewart, "The resurrection of Ralph Nader," pp. 106–10.

3. Tort is defined loosely as injury to one's person, feelings, or reputation or damage to someone's real or personal property.

4. When lawyers agree to take a case on contingency, they are only paid if the case is won. Fees can vary according to individual agreements, but the standard rate is 30 percent of any awards granted.

5. Robert Sherrill, "One Paper that Wouldn't Shut Up; the Insurance 'Crisis' Story," *The Nation*, 17 May 1986, pp. 688–91.

6. Peter Schwartz, "The Moral Menace of Proposition 103," *The Ayn Rand Institute*, http://www.aynrand.org/medialink/prop103.html.

7. Michael Kinsey, "TRB: Saint Ralph," *The New Republic*, 9 December 1985.

8. Quoted in Stewart, "The Resurrection of Ralph Nader," pp. 106–10.

9. Quoted in Stewart, "The Resurrection of Ralph Nader," pp. 106–10.

10. Quoted in David Bollier, *Citizen Action and other Big Ideas, A History of Ralph Nader and the Modern Consumer Movement, Nader.org,* http://www.nader.org/history_bollier. html.

11. Quoted in Jonathan Rowe and Steven Waldman, "Beyond Money: Replacing the Gold Standard with the Golden Rule," *Washington Monthly,* May 1990, pp. 32–40.

12. Quoted in Julie Brienza, "Tort Law Museum Planned by Ralph Nader," *Trial,* July 1998, p. 112.

13. Quoted in Peter Brimelow and Leslie Spencer, "Ralph Nader, Inc." *Forbes,* 17 September 1990, p. 117.

14. *U.S. Tort Costs: 2003 Update, Trends and Finding on the Costs of the U.S. Tort System, Executive Report* (St. Louis, MO: Tillinghast-Towers Perrin) 2003.

15. "A Recession-Resistant Industry, As U.S. Economy Sputters, Trial Lawyers Inc. Continues to Rake It In," *Trial Lawyers, Inc, a Report on the Lawsuit Industry in 2003* (New York: Manhattan Institute for Policy Research), 2003.

16. "A Recession-Resistant Industry, As U.S. Economy Sputters, Trial Lawyers Inc. Continues to Rake It In."

17. "Tillinghast's 'Tort Cost' Figures Vastly Overstate the Cost of the American Legal System," *Americans for Insurance Reform,* 6 January 2004, http://www.insurance-reform.org/pr/Tillinghast_Overstates.pdf.

18. "Our Mission," *Trial Lawyers for Public Justice,* http://www.tlpj.org.

19. Quoted in Brimelow and Spencer, "Ralph Nader, Inc.," pp. 117–25.

20. Rose B. Nader and Nathra Nader, *It Happened in the Kitchen. Recipes for Food and Thought* (Washington, D.C.: Center for Study of Responsive Law, 1991), p. 156.

21. Nader and Nader, *It Happened in the Kitchen: Recipes for Food and Thought,* p. 156.

22. Bollier, *Citizen Action and other Big Ideas, A History of Ralph Nader and the Modern Consumer Movement, Nader.org,* http://www.nader.org/history_bollier. html.

Chapter 10

NADER FOR PRESIDENT?

"What he saw happening was that everything he stood for was being taken away piece by piece," said Marcus Raskin,[1] who had approached Ralph Nader to run in the 1972 election on the New Party ticket; however, Nader had declined. Yet, what Raskin said made sense. For all the years of hard work and the stress involved in fighting the "big guys," Nader was undoubtedly disturbed by the watering down and elimination of what he had helped to accomplish over the years. And true to his form of standing and shouting out his beliefs, Nader accidentally became involved in politics; yet, he was not and would never be a traditional politician.

When the idea arose for Nader to assume the role of third-party candidate, he never expected to win the 1992 election. The whole "campaign" was a sophisticated stunt, devised to allow Nader to spread his message to the people, and it was put into motion with a flippant attitude. Nader would not be on the ballot. He would not be raising funds. No political party endorsed him, and he was not being groomed and prepared by an entourage of personal assistants and advisors. Nader was typically Nader.

"I'm 'none of the above,' and I'm not running for president," he said. "I'm running for a citizen's empowerment agenda."[2] Nader wanted citizens to write him in on the ballot as a protest; and to gain a constituency, he went about stumping all over New Hampshire in an effort to make an impact on the primary election in that state. Many people relished what Nader had to say and came out in support of him. From the time his supporters from around the country showed up in New Hampshire to just a few days before the primary, he had managed to raise $80,000 in campaign contributions without even trying. About 1,000 voters volunteered to help in his campaign.

Still, Nader was reluctant to be a bona fide candidate in the race. "I don't even like saying 'write in Ralph Nader,' but that's the only way we're going to get any attention."[3] He wanted people to hear how the country had become a plutocracy, a government by the wealthy, and how corporations had taken control. He urged people to become responsible citizens and to take back what they already owned, to act as a group of voters, consumers, or taxpayers to build a renewed society. "See how essentially invulnerable these proposals are ideologically?" Nader said. "What are they going to accuse you of, ownershipism?"[4]

After only a short time in the race, Nader was able to convince 2 percent of the New Hampshire voters—more than 3,000 people—to give him their protest votes. Of course, Nader did not win the contest. Republican George H. W. Bush brought in 57 percent of the vote, while on the Democratic side, the winner was Senator Paul Tsongas, with 33 percent of the vote. Other well-known candidates did not fare as well as Nader. Pat Buchanan, who was a serious contender, got only 1,248 votes, and former presidential candidate Eugene McCarthy only brought in 211.

Yet, neither Tsongas nor Bush would ultimately win the presidential election. In a startling 370 electoral vote coup to George H. W. Bush's mere 168 votes, Bill Clinton became the 42nd president of the United States. For the Naderites, this seemed a good change. At last, a Democrat was back in the White House.

BATTLING THE GLOBALIST POWERS

The honeymoon never happened. Clinton and Nader fought several battles over various issues throughout Clinton's tenure. And they never met face-to-face. Nader's characterization of Clinton's administration was sorely negative, "This is the Clinton Administration—an extremely sleazy operation, full of cowards at the top and frustrated decent people at the bottom."[5]

The first major "battle" between the Clintonites and the Naderites was over the North American Free Trade Agreement (NAFTA), and it began even before Clinton ran for office.

President George H. W. Bush was staunchly behind the agreement, and surprisingly, so were many neo-Democrats, like Clinton. The treaty would allow free trade among Canada, the United States, and Mexico, the objectives of which are summarized in the agreement's preamble, which reads:

1. The objectives of this Agreement as elaborated more specifically through its principles and rules, including national treatment, most-favored-nation[6] treatment and transparency, are to:

   a) eliminate barriers to trade in, and facilitate the cross-border movement of goods and services between the territories of the Parties;
   b) promote conditions of fair competition on the free trade area;
   c) increase substantially investment opportunities in the territories of the Parties;
   d) provide adequate and effective protection and enforcement of intellectual property rights in each Party's territory;
   e) create effective procedures for the implementation and application of this Agreement, for its joint administration and for the resolution of disputes; and
   f) establish a framework for further trilateral, regional and unilateral cooperation to expand and enhance the benefits of this Agreement.[7]

President Bush urged Congress to give him the "fast track" authority for NAFTA. In this process, Congress agrees in advance to approve or reject the agreement as a whole, without laboring over amendments. Fast track authority, authorized by the 1974 Trade Act, gives the President the power to make agreements without the fear that they will be unraveled in lengthy Congressional hearings. For NAFTA, fast-track authority was approved.

Though the intention of NAFTA seemed progressive on the surface, Nader and Public Citizen did not see it that way. Nader saw NAFTA as a mechanism for weakening our internal policies for the health and safety of workers in America because certain provisions of the treaty would never be discussed with the public. It was a treaty made by the governments, for the governments, or—as Nader saw it more clearly—a treaty by the corporations, for the corporations. Nader also wondered if the people who voted on the treaty had ever read the voluminous NAFTA agreement and if they understood its implications—corporations would be able to move labor into Mexico, where wages were far below the standards for American workers. This would allow them to produce cheaper goods or more often, secure higher profits

Nader also worried about dealing with Mexico and wrote, "The core question is whether our modest democracy can enter into an economic union with a repressive dictatorial regime, composed of a few very wealthy ruling families, government officials and the police power."[8] And he provided this scenario:

> For example, a U.S. factory closes down in Missouri and goes to Mexico where even weak worker, environmental, tax, and other laws go unenforced. This transplanted factory can then sell its products back into the United States in competition with a factory that stayed in the United States and followed the rules. Under NAFTA, the U.S. government can complain before a secret commission that is structurally unable to make a decision for many months, much less enforce it. Our courts have no role in these matters.[9]

The influx of Mexican workers was inevitable given that the hourly factory wage in the United States at the time was $10.97, but in Mexico was a mere $1.85, according to the Institute for Agriculture and Trade Policy.[10] But the arguments about NAFTA did not begin with the loss of jobs; they began with the environmentalists. There had been no such considerations in the 1988 Canada–United States Free Trade Agreement, which had ignited controversy between the two countries over acid rain from the United States polluting the lakes and trees in Canada.

NAFTA AND THE ENVIRONMENT

When considering the United States, Canada, and Mexico, any treaty involving commerce would affect air pollution, acid rain, and other sources of environmental concern in all three countries. Environmentalists include not only those interested in the preservation of the earth, but also wildlife, conservation of natural resources, and public health hazards. Nader's Public Citizen is one of those organizations, and with other groups, it saw Mexico as the major complication.

President Carlos Salinas de Gotari heavily promoted the NAFTA treaty. As the weakest link in the U.S.–Canada–Mexico chain, he saw it as a vehicle for reconstructing the Mexican economy and agreed that environmental issues had to be addressed in the new agreement and that controls should be modeled after those already in place in the United States. However, there was deep concern over the Mexican ability to enforce those regulations. Mexico had too few to do the policing, insufficient funding, and their laboratories were poorly equipped for proper testing. And unlike the American public's right to take legal action when the regulations were broken, citizens of Mexico had no equivalent rights.

Environmentalists' deep concerns were that the potential increase in production in Mexico, because of NAFTA, would only exacerbate the condition. They pointed to the *maquiladoras*—the Mexican enterprises—already in operation along the U.S.–Mexican border, which were polluting American air and water, and to Mexico City, one of the dirtiest atmospheres on Earth.

The other side of the argument—which included trade economists, American industry, and others—argued that only through the facilitation of trade among the countries would Mexico obtain the necessary resources to clean up its environment. They pointed to the elimination or reduction of tariffs as a curative for the maquiladoras. These enterprises were in the business of temporarily importing American-made products in the rough, duty-free. The maquiladora would add the finishing touches to the products, and when they were returned to American soil, the tariff paid on the finished goods only applied to the low-value improvements made on the Mexican side of the border. With an agreement to require little or no tariffs, the need for the maquiladoras to be so close to the border would be eliminated.

Environmentalists countered with the idea that more American industries would flee to the Mexican side of the border to avoid more stringent American controls. Yet, the economists stated that costs to U.S. industries are a small fraction of the operating budget. Moving their operations to Mexico, just to evade environmental regulations, would not be economically prudent. However, those against NAFTA saw this as little comfort and asserted that corporations, historically unconcerned with the condition of the earth, had instigated the trade agreement. Big business's claims of NAFTA creating many thousands of high-paying American jobs, raising the standard of living in all three countries, and improving environmental conditions appeared to the non-governmental organizations (NGOs) to be a load of hogwash.[11]

Friends of the Earth, the Sierra Club, and Public Citizen filed a case in the U.S. District Court of the District of Columbia. Aside from Bush's assurances and the terms of the proposed NAFTA, the organizations wanted solid proof that the trilateral treaty would not negatively affect the environment. Environmentalists went to the court to force requirement of an environmental impact statement (EPI), and they wanted it to be made part of NAFTA's ratification, stating that NAFTA would "significantly impact the human environment."[12] The same case had been brought to court in November 1991, but was dismissed by the court on the grounds that the trade agreement had not yet been reached. When the new case was filed, Lori Wallach, staff attorney for Public Citizen, said, "An agree-

ment in NAFTA has now been reached, and environmental and consumer health and safety issues have become pivotal in determining [its]
future."[13]

Yet, once again, the environmentalists lost and the governmental EPI
was never filed. This prompted the environmental NGOs to team up with
the more powerful labor faction, which was against NAFTA and the
prospect of losing jobs to Mexico. Labor unions had much bigger influence over Congress, and the two sides hoped to sway legislators away from
approving the treaty.

A REASONABLE CONCESSION?

By September 1993, the three countries came up with an agreement to
allay all environmental concerns. The North American Agreement on
Environmental Cooperation (NAAEC) included provisions for enhance-
ments to and enforcement of environmental laws. The agreement also established a Commission for Environmental Cooperation (CEC), which
would be staffed by cabinet members responsible for environmental protection from each partner in the agreement. The CEC would also be required to file an annual report for public scrutiny each year. Yet, the
procedures for resolving any disputes were so convoluted as to be ridicu-
lous. Annette Baker Fox outlined the process this way:

> Any person or nongovernmental organization could submit a
> complaint to the secretariat that a government of another
> party was failing to enforce its trade-related environmental
> laws. Following specified criteria and guidelines, the secretariat
> would then consider how to proceed. If a persistent pattern
> were discerned, only the governments could establish a panel
> of independent experts...to examine the alleged pattern of
> nonenforcement and propose a remedy. The panel of five
> would be drawn from a roster of forty-five already chosen by
> the council. Two out of the three parties must request setting
> up such a panel, which reassured the weaker members that
> United States companies could not use the system for unwar-
> ranted purposes.[14]

Neither Mexico nor Canada was anxious to frame their trade agreement by linking it to environmental concerns, but each country had its
reasons for wanting the agreement that outweighed these issues. Mexico,
in particular, spent a great deal to ensure the success of the agreement and

ultimately, against all protests, NAFTA was finally signed by the three nations on December 17, 1992.

Several NGOs were convinced that the treaty was dire for the United States and its citizens, and to make the controversy even broader, the antiglobalists (who are set against the idea of a one-world government and see the country becoming increasingly interested in such an arrangement, prompted by big business) were up in arms when President George H. W. Bush said at the agreement's signing, "I hope and trust that the North American free trade area can be extended to Chile, other worthy partners in South America and Central America and the Caribbean. Free trade throughout the Americas is an idea whose time has come. A new generation of democratic leaders has staked its future on that promise. And under their leadership, a tide of economic reform and trade liberalization is transforming the hemisphere."[15]

The ensuing debate in Congress over ratification of the treaty was volatile. Some environmental organizations still opposed the treaty, but others embraced it, including the National Audubon Society, the National Wildlife Federation, the Natural Resources Defense Council, the Environmental Defense Fund, the World Wildlife Federation, and Conservation International. Later, the Sierra Club repudiated its stand in opposition, as well. By this time, Clinton had taken office and a firm stand on the agreement, urging Congress and the nation to accept its terms. "I feel very strongly that it's the right thing and I'm not going to keep plugging away, hoping we can pass it," he said.[16] Neither the anti-NAFTA NGOs nor labor could convince Congress that NAFTA was a bad deal, and the legislation was ratified by Congress and signed as PL 103–182 into law on December 8, 1993, by President Clinton. NAFTA would go into effect on January 1, 1994, to the disappointment of Nader, who had formed a sort of alliance to oppose NAFTA with the unlikely associates Pat Buchanan, Ross Perot, and Jerry Brown, former governor of California.

GATT CONTINUES THE CONTROVERSY

Though this battle for NAFTA was over and lost, the battle over the Uruguay rounds of the General Agreement on Tariffs and Trade (GATT) had already begun. GATT was first signed on October 30, 1947 in the interest of reducing world trade barriers via limiting tariffs on both imports and exports. Leaders from around the world had already held seven rounds of negotiations over the years to refine and improve the original agreement, but in 1986, the Uruguay Round of new GATT regulations came under fire, especially from Nader.

When this round of negotiations began, GATT had no organization behind it. It was simply a multinational agreement. In fact, once the proposed International Trade Organization (ITO) came into business, the participants in GATT had intentions of abandoning GATT and allowing the ITO to govern international trade. Yet, the ITO was so complicated and had so much opposition that Congress never voted on it and the organization never came to fruition, thereby allowing GATT to continue to govern world trade.

The Uruguay round of negotiations took seven years to complete, and in this round, intellectual property trading was brought under the aegis of GATT. The World Trade Organization (WTO) was also established to administer the agreement. President Clinton was firmly behind the Uruguay Round and sought approval from Congress. Opponents of this agreement saw it as a threat to democracy and the institution of the New World Order so much discussed in the previous presidential administration.

Regarding the WTO, Nader wrote in USA Today on November 22, 1994, "You, the readers, would be barred from observing, participating in or appealing any of these tribunals' decisions affecting your health, safety, and workplace conditions."[17] He balked at two mandates of the agreement. The first involved the ascendance of world trade over nontrade issues, such as pollution control, occupational health and safety, tax policies, and food safety. The other was the proposed uniformity of standards. As the United States is foremost in these areas, Nader saw GATT as a negative force on our higher safety regulations.

Nader cited the example of trucking weights. In the United States, the gross vehicle weight of a tractor-trailer could not exceed 80,000 pounds, but Mexico's truck weight standard is 175,000 pounds. Knowing the corporate penchant for using the advantage, Nader asked, "Which image do you think your rear-view mirror will reflect in a few years?"[18]

International trade is a means for growth in the U.S. economy, so GATT did have its proponents, including exporters, certain labor contingents, policymakers, economists, and globalists, and by 1992, the United States had become the world's largest importer and exporter. These pro-GATT groups did not see the arrangement as a loss of sovereignty but, rather, as a means of promoting an international economy and a first step in homogenizing world economic practices and cultures. President Clinton was the chief supporter of the Uruguay Round of the GATT sessions, and he pressed Congress to vote for the trade bargain and the proposed WTO to replace GATT as an international organization to deal with global trade rules among member nations.

The WTO was a major stumbling block. Nader and Public Citizen, among other groups and individuals, feared that WTO practices would take precedence over the domestic policies of the United States, though experts declared the WTO to have no more authority than the GATT, already in place. Still unconvinced were not only Public Citizen and Nader but also the Institute for Agriculture and Trade Policy, columnist Pat Buchanan, and 55 members of Congress from both parties, who urged President Clinton to delay the vote in Congress until July 1995. The debate raged on. Nader said, "When historians look back on this period...either they will focus on it as a moment in which the Congress resisted the antidemocratic WTO or they will view it as the moment in which Congress ceded authority to safeguard the interests of this country and its inhabitants to this new autocratic international body."[19]

Though the WTO would ultimately come to fruition, it was neither the first nor the last time that Clinton and Nader would disagree on serious issues. From Clinton's nomination of Zoe Baird for Attorney General of the United States, when Baird was found to have hired illegal immigrants as domestics in 1993, to Clinton's intended elimination of the Aid to Families with Dependent Children (AFDC) Program, to what Nader perceived to be Clinton's kowtowing to corporate interests, Clinton was not at all the Democrat Nader thought he should be.

THE RELUCTANT CONTENDER

Nader believed that party was not an issue. By 1996, he had begun referring to Clinton and his Republican rival in the 1996 Presidential election, Bob Dole, as "Tweedledee and Tweedledum." In his mind, neither the Democratic nor the Republican parties were for the people, but for the interests of large corporations. Of Clinton, he said, "In the first three years of his tenure, he's been consistently on the side of big business when it's conflicted with labor and consumers."[20]

Nader was also appalled when every proposal brought forward by the Progressive Caucus of the Democratic party's platform committee was rejected, as they could not muster the 15 votes from the 180-member committee needed to bring the proposals to debate. What irked him most is that they were not new ideas, including national health care; elimination of tax breaks to wealthy corporations; a moratorium on the death penalty; fair trade, in which all workers would be treated humanely and provided a proper minimum wage, more stringent environmental controls throughout the trading area, along with democratization of the WTO; opposition to "fast track" authority for the president; and an end to missile defense systems that were costly and not working. Yet, the Progressives could not get more than five votes from the committee to hold further discussion. Though Nader had toyed with the election in 1992, in 1996, his displeasure with the state of the nation, made him part of it.

He would run as a candidate for the Green Party, though he was not a Green. He had made a promise to his father that he would always remain independent, and he has. But in October 1995, he had hinted at himself as a candidate when he told the *Chicago Tribune* that he was eyeing California because of Clinton's wavering on measures of deregulation of securities fraud, legal services, telecommunications, and welfare and that if Clinton did not veto the measures, he was nothing more than a Republican president. With more than 50 votes in the Electoral College, California has historically been an important state in all presidential races. Nader toyed with taking votes from Clinton there. He had an ample approval rating after his success with Proposition 103, and he surmised that he might ruin Clinton's chances for reelection if he became a candidate himself.

A group of Green Party activists, admiring his stance on many issues, wrote to Mr. Nader to ask him to become their candidate in the presidential election. "We are not asking you to commit to running nationally at this time, not to appear on California's 1996 General Election Ballot," the letter read. "Rather the announcement of your appearance on the...primary election ballot will spur grassroots organizing around the country that will determine whether sufficient support exists to make your candidacy nationally viable. Call it the 'modified hang out your shingle' strategy."[21]

Nader eventually agreed to become the Green Party candidate in a win-win situation. The Greens needed someone with name recognition to ignite interest in their third party. Nader was perfect, as he drew interest from a broad spectrum of the population, across party lines. He gave the Greens credibility, softening their perceived persona as "tree huggers."

Nader also benefited from this alliance. The Greens were his ticket to get on the ballot in the only primary state he had designs on campaigning in—California. His aim was to destroy the "duopoly" system of American politics. But why, when he said so many times he would not become a politician, was he entering the primary race?

Nader was irate about Clinton's raising the speed limits above 55 miles per hour. "You know what the death toll was the year after 55 went into effect?" Nader asked. "Nine thousand less. Clinton's killing and injuring tens of thousands of people a year. More air pollution, more imported oil, higher autoworker compensation rates, and $20 billion in health costs. And Clinton doesn't give a shit."[22] With great ire for Clinton's action,

Nader allowed the Greens to put his name on the California primary ballot. He was still only trying to make a point, not to become an elected official. Nader had no intention of running a campaign. "I intend to stand with others around the country as a catalyst for the creation of a new model of electoral politics, not to run any campaign," he said. "I will not seek nor accept any campaign contributions."[23]

SPOILER OR GRASSROOTS HERO?

Most political pundits saw Nader as an election "spoiler." Because of his political views, it was assumed that he would take votes from the Democrats and give Bill Clinton a wake-up call. Estimates gave Nader 5 percent of the vote, allowing Bob Dole, the Republican candidate, the win.

By April 1996, Nader was on the ballot in Maine, New Mexico, and California. And some political analysts had upped their estimates of Nader's success in California to 6 percent of the vote. People began to ask him why he would not seriously consider running for office, when with only 5 percent of the vote, his party would retroactively be eligible for millions in matching federal funds. "You remember when I said I wasn't running for elective office?... Some people have heard me say it 200 times. I don't break that."[24]

Nader did not see himself as a spoiler, either. He thought that he would attract those people who had stopped or never started voting to vote for him, just because he had something new to offer. He wanted to run on a platform of building democracy. He said, "These parties are not offering an adequate choice given their duopoly over politics. Clinton has become George Ronald Clinton: pro the General Agreement on Tariffs and Trade, pro the North Atlantic Free Trade Agreement, giving in to one corporate demand after another, not fighting back and drawing the line against Dole and Gingrich on the deregulation of health and safety agencies."[25]

These words were refreshing to many ears, after decades of dissatisfying leaders. Yet, not all were with Nader, and some accused him of holding back, illegally. They said that because he limited his campaign contributions to $5,000, he would not have to abide by the law requiring candidates to disclose personal financial information. The *Wall Street Journal*, a longtime nemesis of Nader, accused him of hiding the very information that he heckled corporations for in the past and labeled him hypocritical. "The most important disclosure is 'Where did the money come from?'" he said. "My answer is, from nowhere. The rest is self-flagellation. One's [personal finances] should remain private and never be violated. I don't care about other candidates' tax returns."[26]

In the California primary, Nader pulled in 22,649 votes or a mere .045 percent of the vote on May 26, 1996. Though the results were not what the pundits had forecast, the ball was in motion and on August 19, the Greens elected Nader as their candidate in the national election.

For his running mate, Nader chose Winona LaDuke, an Anishinabe (Ojibway) of the Mississippi Band from the White Earth Reservation in Minnesota. LaDuke is also an author, an activist, and the mother of two children. She gave her reasons for running in a speech, which was later reprinted in the *Earth Island Journal.* "I am interested in reframing the debate on the issues of this society—the distribution of power and wealth; the abuse of power; the rights of the natural world; the environment; and the need to consider an amendment to the U.S. Constitution in which all decisions made today will be considered in light of their impact on the seventh generation from now."[27]

Still, there was no formal campaigning and no formal fund raising. Nader and LaDuke would run on principle alone. As Nader took the podium to accept the nomination, the crowd began to chant, "Go, Ralph, go! Go, Ralph, go!" Nader, always uncomfortable when the spotlight is turned on him personally rather than on one of his causes, asked the crowd for silence and said, "The intonation should be, 'Go, *we* go!'"[28] The enthusiasm with which the crowd took up the mantra signified the Greens as a unified voice.

In the end, the Green party secured spots on the ballots in 22 states. Though receiving only 1 percent of the popular vote, the election had given a voice to Nader's causes. What the people did not know was that he was just getting warmed up and that his next foray into the political arena would include a controversy that might never disappear.

NOTES

1. Quoted in Justin Martin, *Nader, Crusader, Spoiler, Icon* (New York: Perseus, 2002), p. 228.

2. Quoted in Micah L. Sifry, "Nader's Progress," *New York,* 17 February 1992, p. 185.

3. Quoted in Marci McDonald, "Ralph Nader's Latest Raid," *Maclean's,* 17 February 1992, p. 24.

4. Quoted in Sifry, "Nader's Progress," p. 185.

5. Quoted in Amy Goodman and Larry Bensky, "Transcript of Pacific Radio Interview with Ralph Nader," *Findlaw.com,* 11 September 1996, http://legal-minds.lp.findlaw.com/list/cyberjournal/msg00131.html.

6. A policy used by the United States that allows for lower tariffs, cooperative trading, and protection from discrimination.

7. "NAFTA Text," *Office of NAFTA and Inter-American Affairs*, http://www.mac.doc. gov/nafta/chapter1.html.

8. Ralph Nader, "NAFTA vs. Democracy," *Multinational Monitor*, October 1993, http://multinationalmonitor.org/hyper/issues/1993/10/mm/1093_02.html.

9. Ralph Nader, "NAFTA vs. Democracy."

10. "NAFTA Fact Check," Multinational Monitor, October 1993, http://multinationalmonitor.org/hyper/issues/1993/10/mm1093_02.html.

11. An NGO is any organization not affiliated with the United States government.

12. Virginia Gannon, "Three Groups Sue to Force Free-Trade Pact Study," *American Metal Market*, 22 September 1992, p. 4.

13. Quoted in Gannon, "Three Groups Sue to Force Free-Trade Pact Study," p. 4.

14. Annette Baker Fox, "Environment and Trade: The NAFTA Case Contributors," *Political Science Quarterly*, 1995, pp. 49–68.

15. President George H. W. Bush, Remarks on signing the North American Free Trade Agreement, *"Weekly Compilation of Presidential Documents,"* 21 December 1992, pp. 2363–2366.

16. Quoted in "Clinton Says NAFTA Will be a Tough Fight," *Trade News Bulletin*, 3 June 1993, http://www.etext.org/Politics.Trade.News/Volume.2/tnb-02.098.

17. Ralph Nader, "Reject This Flawed Treaty," USA *Today*, 22 November 1994, reprinted in Ralph Nader, *The Ralph Nader Reader* (New York: Seven Stories Press, 2000), p. 197.

18. Nader, "Reject This Flawed Treaty," p. 198.

19. Quoted in Susan Aaronson, "The Policy Battle over Freer World Trade," *Challenge*, 1994, pp. 48–64.

20. Quoted in *All Politics*, "Ralph Nader Says He'll Challenge Clinton in California in November," *CNN.com*, http://www.cnn.com/ALLPOLITICS/1996/news/9603/24/nader/index.shtml.orig.

21. Quoted in Micah L. Sifry, "Nader's Green Light," *The Nation*, 8 January 1996, p. 6.

22. Quoted in James Ridgeway, "The Reluctant Candidate," *The Village Voice*, 12 December 1995, p. 25.

23. Quoted in Ridgeway, "The Reluctant Candidate," p. 25.

24. Quoted in Sifry, "Nader's Green Light," p. 7.

25. Quoted in Patrick Small, "Holy Ralph's Biggest Crusade," *New Statesman*, 30 August 1996, pp. 16–17.

26. Quoted in Maria Armoudian, "A Little Green: Shaky Start for the Nader Campaign," *The Progressive*, October 1996, p. 28.

27. Winona LaDuke, "Why I Chose to Run," *Earth Island Journal*, Fall 1996, p. 42.

28. Quoted in Greta S. Gaard, *Ecological Politics: Ecofeminists and the Greens*. (Philadelphia, PA: Temple University Press, 1998), p. 241.

Chapter 11

NOT JUST ANOTHER CANDIDATE

When Ralph Nader chose to run for president in 1996, people were amazed that he reversed a Nader decision. He had shunned any kind of political involvement until his 1992 noncampaign for president, staged strictly to show the country's unwavering dedication to a two-party system that does not work. But in 2000, Nader had become more serious. This time, he was in it to win and actively sought votes. But why this time? Why were things different?

Nader had encouraged talk-show host Phil Donahue to run for the U.S. Senate seat in Connecticut in 1998. For decades, Donahue had tackled issues of women's rights, abortion, campaign reform, and many other substantial societal issues on his talk show. Though passionate about his views, Donahue was always known for giving the other side a say, and it was no secret that he was fed up with the American political system. Nader thought him to be the perfect candidate for the Senate seat, but Donahue had declined. "His polite refusal further fueled my sense that those of us striving for a [sic] clean politics could no longer be on the sidelines and self-indulgently recoil from diving in to be members of the cleaning crew."[1]

Nader also saw increasingly universal control of politics, economics, and society in general by corporations. Many politicians were beholden to them for sizable campaign contributions and so generally voted in the corporate interest. Americans lost jobs, as Nader and others had predicted would happen in the wake of the North American Free Trade Agreement (NAFTA) and the General Agreement on Tariffs and Trade (GATT). Advertising, directed toward children, ensured a new generation of consumers, anxious to try every new product they saw, and the corporate impact upon the environment extended far beyond the borders of the United States. Nader wrote of big business, "Indeed, in their largest and most transnational form, the global corporations reject allegiance to nation or community."[2]

Late in December 1999, Nader gathered some respected advisors to discuss a campaign. He was alarmed at the Commission on Presidential Debates (CPD), which regulates the manner in which presidential debates are held and, more importantly, which candidates are permitted to participate. Though Nader planned to visit all 50 states if he ran, he knew that the number of people he would be able to reach in each state would be limited. The debates are nationally televised and attract millions of viewers, giving an incredible edge to those candidates who are able to take part. He saw his participation in the debates as the keystone in his campaign.

The CPD is a private corporation that was organized in 1987 by the Republican and Democratic parties. "Its primary purpose is to sponsor and produce debates for the United States leading presidential and vice presidential candidates and to undertake research and educational activities relating to the debates,"[3] the Commission states on its Web site. Nader wonders about the veracity of the statement because he accuses the CPD of being beholden to corporate interest. Indeed, the CPD gives credit to major corporations for aiding in its web presence—Oracle, AT&T, 3Com, and Harris Interactive are mentioned, along with other familiar web companies. However, its board of directors lists Caroline Kennedy, former Senator John C. Danforth, and Mexican American's Education and Legal Defense Fund's Antonia Hernandez, along with Warren Buffet, CEO of Berkshire Hathaway, Inc.; Frank J. Fahrenkopf, Jr., president and CEO of the American Gaming Association; and Paul G. Kirk Jr., a director of Hartford Financial Services, Inc. Nader cites other corporations who contribute to the CPD—Ford Motors, Philip Morris, and Anheuser Busch, among other well-recognized names. His contention is that the CPD is purely a mechanism to keep third-party candidates from participating in the debates.

The CPD applies three criteria to determine a candidate's worthiness to appear in any debate:

- Evidence of Constitutional Eligibility: the candidate must be at least 35 years of age, be a natural born citizen of the United States.

- Evidence of Ballot Access: For a candidate to appear on enough state ballots that he or she has a mathematical chance of winning enough electoral votes to secure the presidency, which would be 270 electoral votes.

- Indicators of Electoral Support: As determined by an average of five national polling organizations, at least a 15 percent approval ratio from the national electorate, to be determined by the most recent statistics at the time of calculation.

Nader sees this third criterion as a paradox because the polling companies in question are owned by at least three major media corporations, such as the *New York Times, CNN,* and the *Washington Post,* and because none cover third-party campaigns, that there would be little chance of gaining the required poll ratings. And to make it a real Catch-22 situation, because a third-party candidate did not climb high enough in the polls, the media would see no reason for adequate campaign coverage. Ergo, the circuitous discriminatory plan is complete. To make it more obvious that third-party candidates would not be welcome in any election year 2000 debates, co-chairmen of CPD—Fahrenkopf, a Republican, and Kirk, a Democrat—announced at a January 6 press conference that the 15 percent average had to be attained by September 2000 for any candidate wishing to participate in the debates.

THE SLATE

Nearing the beginning of 2000, the Republican candidates were in a heated race between Texas Governor George W. Bush and Senator John McCain of Arizona. On the Democratic side were former Senator Bill Bradley from New Jersey and incumbent Vice President Al Gore. Nader was not the only non-institutional party candidate. Columnist Pat Buchanan was running on the Reform Party ticket.

Though the Republican race was heady, it was evident that George W. Bush was the Republican hierarchy's choice. McCain, a former Vietnam POW, who rejected the Vietnamese offer to go free until all of his men could be released with him, seemed to have strength of character to Nader. Yet, some of his issues were not Nader-oriented, such as being pro-life on the abortion issue, pro WTO, and pro-death penalty. Nader said in a *Meet the Press* interview, "I don't think government has the proper role in forcing a woman to have a child or forcing a woman not to have a child. ... This is something that should be privately decided with the family, [the] woman, [and] all the other private factors of it, but we should work toward preventing the necessity of abortion."[4] McCain, on the other hand, said, "As a leader of a pro-life party with a pro-life position, I will persuade young Americans [to] understand the importance of the preservation of the rights of the unborn."[5]

George W. Bush—son of George H. W. Bush, the 41st president of the United States, and grandson of Prescott Bush, who was a senator from Connecticut from 1952 to 1963—was the governor of Texas when the 2000 presidential race was underway. Nader thought that McCain should have won the hearts and minds of the people, but that the race was decided before it began. Nader wrote, "So why didn't he win the nomination? Because the Republican Party politicos, along with key Republican governors in key primary states, had already chosen Bush."[6]

Nader and Bush disagreed on several issues—abortion, civil rights, the death penalty, and the environment, among others. One of their major disagreements was in reforming the tort system and the courts. "From people across America," Bush said, "I am hearing that our legal system needs reform. That our courts aren't servicing the people, they are serving the lawyers. That frivolous lawsuits are hurting people. Some think this special interest group is too powerful to take on. That money determines everything. This is not an argument; it is an excuse."[7] Nader's position on tort reform was quite clear by that time. He supported consumers' right to fight injustices in the court system and opposed limits to awards given them for actual and punitive damages.

For the Democrats, Bill Bradley had been a U.S. senator, so he knew the ropes in Washington, D.C. He had also been a professional basketball player during the 1970s, when he led the New York Nicks to two NBA titles. And he had played for Nader's alma mater, Princeton. He and Nader agreed on a woman's right to choose whether or not to have an abortion, on cutting the defense budget, and on investing in education. Bradley did however, see the continuation of the death penalty as fitting and thought there should be more trade organizations, such as NAFTA and GATT, whereas Nader opposed the death penalty and globalization.

Then, there was Al Gore. Already in office, he was almost a certain shoe-in for the party's nomination. Like Nader, he was pro-choice, big on education, and had always been touted as an environmentalist. Yet, like Bradley, he saw open trade with foreign nations as important, while he wanted to see environmental controls and labor as part of any negotiations. With this, he and Nader could agree. In fact, their views were similar in several areas; however, Nader saw Gore as part of the status quo, which to him was corporate-sponsored government.

Pat Buchanan, the Reform Party candidate, was conservative in his views for the country. He not only wanted the death penalty, he wanted an immediacy applied: "If [the criminal] was of sound mind, prosecute him, convict him, put him in the electric chair, and send a message to the whole country within a matter of weeks: If this happens again, that's exactly what's going to happen to you."[8] Nader feels quite differently and told CNN, "The death penalty has been shown, in study after study, not to deter homicides; it has been shown to be discriminatorily applied to the poor and the defenseless, especially defendants who don't have lawyers who stay awake at trial."[9]

DIVING INTO UNFAMILIAR WATERS

Seeing no candidate that he could support, Nader jumped into the fray on February 21, 2000 with the aim of returning government to the people, rather than allowing government to continue in its role of corporate pawn. The campaign slogan was "Nader 2000: Government of, by, and for the people...not monitored interests."[10] And he jumped into the Green candidate pool along with three other Green Party hopefuls, including Jello Biafra, lead singer for the Dead Kennedys band.

The Green party's aim was not only to have their candidate elected, regardless of the slimness of a chance for a third party candidate to win an election, but they wanted to build the party by means of attaining government backing for their candidates in the form of matching funds. The rule to obtain this money from the U.S. Treasury seems simple. Candidates must raise a least $5,000 in each of twenty states in denominations of $250 or less. Nader dislikes fund raising, and wrote, "Not since I was a schoolboy swallowing cod liver oil before leaving for school did I have such a taste in my mouth as when I started dialing for dollars."[11]

Yet, there was more than money to consider for a third party to be recognized. They would have to obtain thousands of signatures in each state to get on the ballot with varying requirements among states. Maryland, for instance, requires 1 percent of all voters in the state to sign, which amounts to nearly 40,000 signatures in that one state alone, and in California, there are about 15 million registered voters, making the required 1 percent about 150,000. Texas requires the signatures to be gathered in just 75 days. There was much work to be done, and many eager volunteers needed to do it. In conjunction with these stringent requirements, Nader's team filed nine lawsuits over one detail or another in various states. The results were mixed, but the team did win some victories, and Nader managed to make it onto the ballot in 43 states, but Nader could not appear on the ballots in Georgia, Idaho, Indiana, North Carolina, Oklahoma, South Dakota, or Wyoming.

Nader did not allow the hassle over the ballot issues to deter him from campaigning in all 50 states, however. He made a pledge to do just that and began his travels at the L.A. Press Club. He brought up many of his issues during his speech, including campaign finance reform, the duopoly existing in American politics, and public ownership of the airwaves. During questioning by the press, he brought out the most important issue to his campaign.

> The central contention of politics should be the distribution of power. That is where a political campaign should be first and foremost. The most important question that a candidate can ask the people during the campaign is, "Do you want to be more powerful as a voter, citizen, consumer, worker, taxpayer, and small saver-investor? Or do you want to continue to be rolled and dominated and manipulated by the concentration of power and wealth in too few hands who then establish the supremacy of the political economy over the majority of the people in this country?"[12]

From California, Nader moved to New Mexico, Texas, and other states, including Minnesota, where he met up with then Governor Jesse Ventura. Ventura had been a pro wrestler before he became a politician. His down-to-earth style was the breath of fresh air that Minnesotans had been looking for; however, just as in California in 2004 when Arnold Schwarzenegger seemed an unlikely victor in that gubernatorial recall race, no one really believed that Ventura would be elected in 1998. Nader had to ask what had made the governor's election possible.

DEBATES ARE ALL OF IT

Ventura told Nader that nearing the time of the election, he was running only at about 10 percent in the polls, when he managed to get on 10 statewide debates with the other candidates. He was also fortunate to have been a Minnesotan. In that state, campaigns find adequate resources through public funding to run for election, and there is same-day voter registration. Soon, Ventura found himself going from 10 to 38 percent in the polls, and because he had managed to get reluctant or first-time voters to the polls and have them register and vote on the same day, he was able to garner enough support to win the election.

This fed right into Nader's own beliefs. He calls himself a "Brandeis brief" type person, referring to Louis Dembitz Brandeis, a former Supreme Court Justice and graduate of Harvard Law, Nader's alma mater. In 1908, Brandeis, already known for defending the public interest, was charged with preparing a brief for the state of Oregon, which had just passed laws establishing a 10-hour workday for women. Business owners had attacked the law stating that the law had no relevance for women's health or safety, and Brandeis was out to prove that the law had merit, based in reality. The brief that he prepared for the case was extraordinary in that he cited legal precedent for his argument in the opening 2 pages, but in the 100 to follow, he included psychological, physiological, and economic data regarding the effect on women's health. The work is referred to in legal circles as "The Brandeis Brief," and in addition to winning the case for Oregon, it became the model for all lawsuits involving social and political conditions.

Nader said, "I am a 'Brandeis brief' type of person who believes that factual reality counts, that candidates' records matter greatly, that arguments need to be rooted in evidence, and that robust debates with challenging reporters provide the most level playing fields."[13] This made debate his most valuable tool. Yet, the requirements were so stringent that Nader's participation in the debates was doubtful.

But the first consideration was being officially nominated as the Green Party candidate. On the weekend of June 23, Nader would be at the Renaissance Hotel in Denver, expecting to gain the nomination and hoping for as much press coverage as possible. Reporters from the *Wall Street Journal* came, as did representatives of the *New York Times* and even the foreign press, as the Green Party has branches in many foreign countries. Green members from five different continents came to participate in the proceedings. At the press conference held on the morning of June 24, Nader told the media, "I completed my fifty state tour of the United States. . . . I have come away from this tour with the distinct feeling that America wants a change—a change from the dominance of the two major political parties which offer little more than band-aids for the nation's problems of health, child poverty, job security, and a multitude of other ills that linger from election to election without a solution."[14]

Winona LaDuke, who was nursing a newborn baby at the time, spoke the night before in the Renaissance Hotel ballroom. "I am somebody who believes that cultural diversity is as important as biodiversity," she said. Later in her speech, she brought out the rich versus poor issue. "Public policies in this country should not be written for the richest people, but for the poorest."[15]

The Green Party convention was far different from the accepted parties' gatherings. At Democratic and Republican gatherings, one might find hospitality suites for corporations; free items, emblazoned with advertising, for any party member who wants them; and fundraising among the different corporate groups. The Green party is proud of its lack of corporate ties. Green Party signage was far different from the major conventions, as well. Rather than holding up signs for their candidate of choice, Green signs tend to promote causes regarding the environment or other social issues.

After a few opening speeches, including the keynote speech by radio host, columnist, and author Jim Hightower, Nader began his remarks with, "Welcome to the politics of joy and justice."[16] Two other candidates also spoke to the crowd. Jello Biafra of the Dead Kennedys, a punk rock band said, "This is a very long-term movement, with people of all ages, stripes and designs totally fed up with a corporate monarchy. Our constitutional democracy has slowly but surely been overthrown in a sugar-coated Disney-crusted coup."[17] Stephen Gaskin helped to found The Farm in Tennessee—the biggest hippie commune in the world during the late 1960s into the 1970s, with some 1,300 members—and commented on the change in values existent in American society at that time. "The rules have changed: Bill Clinton's got it so you can go have oral sex and you ain't having sex, and you can smoke pot and, if you don't inhale, you ain't smoking pot."[18] Clearly, this was an interesting group of candidates.

THE GREEN LIGHT

However, Nader and LaDuke had the race sewed up when they hit the conference. After an endorsement of Nader by Hightower, the voting began. Nader and LaDuke garnered 295 votes, while Gaskin and Biafra received only 10 votes each. Nader began his acceptance speech with a very long sentence that resounded throughout the room:

> On behalf of all Americans who seek a new direction, who yearn for a new birth of freedom to build the just society, who see justice as the great work of human beings on Earth, who understand that community and human fulfillment are mutually reinforcing, who respect the urgent necessity to wage peace, to protect the environment, to end poverty and to preserve values of the spirit for future generations, who wish to build a deep democracy by working hard for a regenerative pro-

gressive politics, as if people mattered—to all these citizens and the Green vanguard, I welcome and am honored to accept the Green Party nomination for President of the United States.[19]

Since the nomination was sewn up, the next project of Nader's campaign was getting into the presidential debates, since he needed them to make any kind of showing in the presidential race. Ross Perot had been proof of that in 1992. An entrepreneur, who had come into the presidential race with a great deal of his own money to finance a campaign, was a different voice. He managed to get into the presidential debates and to win a large following of the population. When it was evident that he could not win, but only help George H. W. Bush into another term, he dropped out of the race and supported Bill Clinton. Yet, he still got 19 percent of the popular vote.

In September, Nader tried another tactic to sidestep the CPD. He wrote to major industrial union heads, asking them to bond together to sponsor more debates with an emphasis on labor. Yet, not one labor leader responded, so he tried the civil rights organizations in Southern California, also without result. And without media support, which he was not getting due to low polls, which were low because he was not getting enough ink—another egg/chicken situation—he still had no chance of being included in the CPD debates.

Nader's pro-active stance was to go directly to the people, as he had done for more than two decades. He managed to secure spots on TV talk shows, the first being Bill Maher's *Politically Incorrect* and in the process secured the host's vote. He also went on the *Tonight Show* with Jay Leno, David Letterman's *CBS Late Show*, and made a fourth visit to *Saturday Night Live*. He had no response from *Oprah*, but did visit the *Queen Latifah Show* and the *Charlie Rose Show*.

Then, his campaign came up with an ad, poking fun at the MasterCard ads, which caused an uproar and legal action. The ad began with the presidential "Hail to the Chief," and a male voice said, "Grilled tenderloin for fundraiser: $1,000 a plate," and continued to give examples of exorbitant spending. Then, the music stopped, and the voice continued, "Finding out the truth: Priceless."[20] Afterward, a pitch was made to vote for Nader and the commercial ended.

MasterCard did not appreciate the ad, saying that it infringed on their "Priceless" ad campaign and that by using these ads, Nader was trying to connect his candidacy with MasterCard. The irony is that Nader abhors credit cards and said, "I believe credit card charges are an outrageous fleecing of consumers, lead to invasions of consumer privacy and are used by too many merchants, who threaten damages to credit ratings, to stifle legitimate consumer complaints."[21] He considered them to be political satire, akin to *Saturday Night Live* performances and thought MasterCard's $5 million dollar lawsuit to be ridiculous. He said, "Let me assure Master-Card's executives that the last thing I want consumers to believe is that my campaign is in the business of selling credit cards."[22]

The turmoil surrounding the legal action probably helped Nader, as it gave him media coverage that he otherwise would not have had, and as it turned out, a New York judge denied MasterCard's motion for a temporary restraining order on finding insufficient evidence that Nader's ad would cause the credit card company to suffer any damages if the spots continued to run, and so they did.

STAYING IN THE PUBLIC EYE

Nader continued his round of television appearances with shows like CNN's *Crossfire* and *Talk Back Live*. He also earned spots in print with well-read publications, such as the *Village Voice, Business Week,* and *Time*. The most-asked question was about Nader's campaign taking votes away from Al Gore, by then the Democratic presidential candidate, thus allowing George Bush, the officially nominated Republican candidate, to win. Nader's response was that no candidate was automatically entitled to anyone's vote, but that candidates had to earn votes.

Nader needed to earn votes quickly to rise in the polls and have the required backing to enter the presidential debates, so he tried to cover all the bases and traveled extensively via coach-class airline tickets. In 1971, he had started the Aviation Consumer Action Project to represent the rights of airline passengers, and had flown coach for 40 years. He wrote, "If Gore and Bush had spent more time in coach class, perhaps consumer and safety complaints about air travel would become a priority for the FAA."[23] He scoffed at their use of private jets to avoid the travails of commercial airline passengers throughout their campaigns.

By mid-summer, Nader's polls were running between three and seven percent, which were not enough to get him into the debates. He needed a tremendous boost, but was doing all that was Naderly possible, exceeding most human endurance. Two lawyers, Greg Kafoury and Mark McDougal with their friend Laird Hastay conceived an idea to heighten the campaign. They wanted to launch a round of "super rallies" to fill large auditoriums and stadiums, as they knew Nader was a big draw for the crowds. At first, Nader's campaign leaders, including Campaign Manager Theresa

Amato, were concerned about the expense. Yet, they knew the campaign needed the extra momentum.

When Kafoury, McDougal, and Hastay eventually got the green light from Nader's people, they booked the Portland Memorial Coliseum, which holds 10,000 people and cost the campaign $65,000 to rent for one night. The rally would be held on August 25 and as it was already August 5, the team would have only 20 days to fill the stadium. The cost of the rally had severely depleted their funding.

Nader had worked with citizen groups in Oregon in the past with excellent results, and he felt that many people in Oregon would be behind him. Yet, by the afternoon of August 25, only about 6,000 tickets had been sold and just before the rally began many seats were still empty. Winona LaDuke spoke first, calling for preservation of our national forests and using dams to save salmon, recovering the Great Plains and of bringing back buffalo there. The mother of three received a rousing ovation. When Nader walked onto the stage, it was amidst a shower of energy and enthusiasm and every seat in the house was filled, yet he still couldn't get the necessary backing to participate in the debates.

The first presidential debate of 2000 was held in Boston at the Clark Athletic Center, and Nader had a ticket, not for inside the center, but for Lipke Auditorium, where people could watch the debate on closed-circuit television. After the debate, he was to be interviewed by Fox News, but instead was met by two men in police uniforms and a state trooper, who claimed to represent the CPD. The trooper told Nader that it mattered not that he had a ticket; he would not be allowed admittance. A few words were exchanged, and the state trooper threatened Nader with arrest.

During the third debate, Nader was to be interviewed by WUTV, the student television station of Washington University in St. Louis, Missouri, where the debate was held. His staff acquired perimeter passes to do the interview in a building far from where the actual debate took place and though wearing the passes, he was blocked once again by a policeman who took his arm and forced him back, saying he would not be permitted to enter, though his associates were allowed to proceed. That same day, he filed a lawsuit against the CPD in Boston's federal district court for violating his civil rights.

SUPER RALLIES AND SURPRISING OPPONENTS

The debates were over. If Nader wanted to make a showing in the race, it was imperative that he continue with his grassroots efforts. The Port-

land rally had been so successful that Nader and company wound up conducting more than a dozen super rallies around the country. Though the
Portland rally presenters included only local politicians, celebrities took
notice of Nader's efforts and signed on to perform or speak at the rallies to
follow. Phil Donahue became the Master of Ceremonies. Eddie Vedder of
Pearl Jam, punk diva Patti Smith, and singer Ani Defranco, Jello Biafra,
and Ben Harper of Ben Harper and the Innocent Criminals joined in to
provide musical interludes to the rallies. Actors Tim Robbins, Susan
Sarandon, and Bill Murray lent their support, and speakers Jim Hightower
and Michael Moore added humor. Nader and LaDuke spoke on the issues
to round out the hours- long rallies, the largest of which was in Madison
Square Garden in New York on October 13.

But all the hoopla and public support wasn't getting Nader the needed
polling statistics to allow him to succeed in gaining matching funds for
the Greens, let alone win the presidential race. Many people who wanted
to vote for Nader thought that their votes would be null, since Nader had
no chance to win the election. They worried that voting for Nader was a
vote for Bush, as more of Naders' followers were Democrat than Republican. Yet, Nader did not allow the polls to stop him. Aside from wanting to
have his issues heard, and he was getting the word out, the Green Party
hoped to achieve the needed support to get government funding for the
next election, just as they had hoped to do in 1996.

Gloria Steinem, longtime women's rights activist and founder of Ms.
magazine, was in an uproar about the Nader campaign. A staunch Democrat, Steinem had worked on the presidential campaigns of Adlai Steven-
son in the 1950s and George McGovern in the 1970s and saw Nader's
campaign as detrimental to the race. Her e-mail letter, "Top 10 Reasons
Why I'm Not Voting for Nader (Any One of Them Would Be Enough),"
echoed throughout cyberspace in October, citing his not wanting to run
to become president, but only to gain matching funds for the Green Party
as number ten, all the way to number one, "The art of behaving ethically
is behaving as if everything we do matters. If we want Gore and not Bush
in the White House, we have to vote for Gore and not Bush—out of re-
spect for the vote and self-respect."[24] Steinem's attack confounded Nader,
who could claim work in the area of workplace discrimination and his
founding of a leading women's policy group in the early 1970s. Nader and
Steinem had usually fought on the same side. Yet, Steinem's wasn't the
only attack Nader suffered from those he considered colleagues and
friends.

Twelve of Nader's old Raiders, led by Gary Sellers who had worked on
the mining issue and the Occupational Health and Safety Act (OSHA)

with Nader, formed a group called "Nader's Raiders for Gore." Though Sellers had attended Nader's campaign kick-off in February and had a positive reaction to Nader's candidacy, in August he attended a fundraiser in Washington D.C. and voiced concerns over the Greens undermining Gore. At that time, Nader assured him that his campaign was a fifty-state effort and that the Greens were not going out of their way to target swing states, which had no historical majority in any political party and which could go either Democratic or Republican in terms of electoral votes. Nader wrote, "In the last month or so [of the campaign], Sellers became a Gore servant possessed—mischaracterizing what I had said…about Gore's record and my fifty-state campaign."[25]

The press then joined in, urging Nader to drop out of the race. Anthony Lewis wrote an open letter to Nader in the New York Times, asking if Nader was serious about there being no major differences between Bush and Gore. Robert F. Kennedy, Jr. wrote an op-ed piece for the same paper, in which he attacked Nader with what Nader saw as erroneous information. And the diatribes continued. Frank Barney in The Gay and Lesbian Review Worldwide chimed in with an aside that voting for Nader would assure a Bush win, while in the St. Petersburg Times, columnist Bill Maxwell wrote referring to Nader's monkish image, "Is Nader so 'good' that he and his supporters are willing to put an unqualified person in the White House, a man who will determine the future that they ostensibly put so much stock in?"[26]

The fact that Democrats did not want George W. Bush in the White House was strong. Although the Clinton presidency was fraught with immorality, the economy seemed to be in good shape. People were working and money was flowing like water. Of course most people who aren't involved in the financial industry don't recognize the 10-year cycle. There are five years of credit grantors pushing every credit card, mortgage, and car loan they can on consumers, worthy or not-so-worthy, and then, the companies spend the other five years collecting what they lent. During those five years, credit is tight, people are out of work and the economy is generally in the tank. Though Clinton was credited with prosperity, it was just the natural corporate cycle playing out. Still, folks wanted it to continue and felt that Gore was the key to their continued complacence.

ONLINE ANTICS

Those who looked upon a vote for Nader as a vote for Bush heard Nader's words and agreed that the country needed his type of leadership, rather than the same corporate puppets the country had seen for decades. Yet, the party was in full swing. No one wanted a Republican in the White House.

Then, along came the Internet gurus with a plan to alleviate voters' worries. Two Web sites, www.NaderTrader.org and www.VoteSwap2000 offered those wavering the chance to swap their vote for Nader with a vote for Gore in any of the swing states. In exchange, voters would vote for Gore in states where Bush was the clear frontrunner. The creator of NaderTrader, Jeff Cardille, a 33-year-old graduate student at the University of Wisconsin in Madison, claimed to have received 37,000 visitors in only a few days of being launched, and other sites quickly sprang up. Jim Cody, who founded VoteSwap2000 with Ten Johnson, said, "We did it to see what would happen."[27] They got their results when, about a week later, they posted this message to their site: "We have just received word from the California secretary of state that offering to 'broker the exchange of votes' is a violation of California state law."[28] All but one site was closed down for tampering with the election. Nader and his campaign did not endorse the sites. "I think it's imaginative, but it's frivolous and diversionary," Nader replied. "You should vote your conscience."[29]

In the end, Nader came in third, gaining 2.74 percent of the popular vote, or 2,882,955 votes. Though his campaign fell far short of the needed five percent for matching funds for the Green party, Nader's views had come before the public, arousing interest in all corners of the country. Perhaps many wanted to vote for Nader, but secretly changed their minds when it came time to pull the lever or punch the chad. Yet, the election did not end on November 5, 2000, and for Nader, the hassle had only begun.

NOTES

1. Ralph Nader, *Crashing the Party* (New York: St. Martin's Press, 2002), p. 123.

2. Nader, *Crashing the Party*, p. xiii.

3. *Commission on Presidential Debates*, http://www.debates.org/index.html.

4. Ralph Nader, "Transcript: Ralph Nader on *Meet the Press*, Sunday, May 7, 2000," *Common Dreams News Center*, 5 May 2000, http://www.commondreams.org.

5. Quoted in "John McCain on Abortion," *Issues 2000, Every Presidential Candidates' View on Every Issue*, 26 January 2000, http://www.issues2000.org/2000/John_McCain_ Abortion.htm.

6. Nader, *Crashing the Party*, p. 60.

7. George W. Bush, "Renewing America's Purpose, Policy Address of George W. Bush, July 1999 to July 2000," *Issues 2000*, http://www.issues2000.org/Purpose.htm.

8. "Pat Buchanan on MSNBC's *Equal Time*," quoted on *Issues 2000*, 2 November 1999, http://www.issues2000.org/2000/pat_Buchanan_Crime.htm.

9. Ralph Nader, "CNN: 'Burden of Proof,'" *Issues 2000*, 9 August 2000, http://www.issues2000.org/2000/Ralph_Nader_Crime.htm.

10. "Ralph Nader on Corporations," *Green Party of Illinois*, http://www.greens.org/illinois/flyers/Corporations.pdf.

11. Nader, *Crashing the Party*, p. 66.

12. Ralph Nader, "The Central Contention of Politics Should Be the Distribution of Power," *Speech to the Los Angeles Press Club*, March 1, 2000, http://www.ratical.org/co-globalize/RalphNader/030100.html.

13. Nader, *Crashing the Party*, p. 100.

14. Anonymous, "Ralph Nader and Winona LaDuke Arrive at the Green Convention in Denver," *Green Campaign 2000*, http://www.greens.org/colorado/pressrelease10.html.

15. Anonymous, "Ralph Nader and Winona LaDuke Arrive."

16. Nader, *Crashing the Party*, p. 149.

17. Quoted in Cara DeGete, "The Green Team," *Colorado Springs Independent*, 29 June 2000, http://www.csindy.com/csindy/2000–06–29/cover.html.

18. Quoted in Cara DeGete, "The Green Party's 2000 National Convention in Denver," *Colorado Springs Independent*, 29 June 2000, http://www.csindy.com/csindy/ 2000–06–29/cover.html.

19. Ralph Nader, "Acceptance Statement of Ralph Nader," *Vote Nader.org*, 25 June 2000, http://www.votenader.org/press/000625acceptance_speech.html.

20. Northwoods Advertising, "Priceless Truth," *Democracy in Action*, 7 August 2000, http://www.gwu.edu/~action/ads2/nadead1.html.

21. Katharine Mieszkowski, "Nader to MasterCard: 'Lighten Up,'" Salon, 18 August 2000, http://dir.salon.com/business/feature/2000/08/18/nader_mastercard/index.html.

22. "Nader: 'Priceless Ads Will Run Despite MasterCard suit," *CNN.com*, 17 August 2000, http://www.cnn.com/2000/ALLPOLITICS/stories/08/17/nader.story/.

23. Nader, *Crashing the Party*, p. 153.

24. Gloria Steinem, "Top Ten Reasons Why I'm Not Voting for Nader (Any One of Which Would be Enough)" http://dpsinfo.com/women/steinem.html.

25. Nader, *Crashing the Party*, p. 244.

26. Bill Maxwell, "Nader's Wrongly Imposed Morality," *St. Petersburg Times*, 25 October 2000, p. 17.A.

27. Quoted in Anonymous, "Let's make a deal: Nader, Gore Supporters Propose Swapping Votes," *Florida Times Union*, 29 October 2000, p. A.19.

28. Quoted in Eugene Kiely, "Nader's Traders? A Swap Meet of Voters," *Philadelphia Inquirer*, 31 October 2000, http://search.epnet.com/direct.asp?an=2W72667410602&db= nfh.

29. Quoted in Christine Cupaiuolo, "When a Personal Vote Isn't Personal, ACLU, National Voting Rights Institute Challenge Vote-Swap Decisions in Court," *PopPolitics.com*, 2 November 2000, http://www.poppolitics.com/articles/2000–11–02-nadergorelegal. shtml.

Chapter 12

MARCHING TOWARD
THE FUTURE

"You can't spoil a system spoiled to the core," Nader said the day after the election.[1] He had been defending his candidacy throughout, but something happened in Florida, a state that is rich with 25 electoral votes. The president is elected through the Electoral College of voters, who represent each state, so Florida was a big block of votes when questing for the needed 210 electoral votes to gain the presidency. Yet, Nader received only 2 percent of the popular vote. How could he have made a difference?

Both Bush and Gore commanded 49 percent of the vote when all the precincts were in, and because the race was so close, Florida law mandated a recount. The source of contention was not so much with re-tally, but with the questionable method of voting in some 26 Florida counties. Palm Beach County voters complained about the complexity of the "butterfly ballot," which opened in book form. Each candidate was listed on either side of the ballot and the voters were expected to punch a hole in the appropriate spot for their choice, in the form's center. Voters voiced their concerns that it was very hard to distinguish which candidate corresponded with which hole in the ballot. Some of the ballots were not punched properly and had hanging chads, which were the tiny bits of paper remaining after holes were punched. Some ballots had attempts at punching, but were only "dimpled" or even termed "pregnant." Some ballots were punched to vote for both candidates and the same types of errors were found in several other counties. Both candidates sent teams of lawyers to Florida as the Gore campaign asked for a hand recount of ballots, rather than a machine recount, in four counties: Palm Beach, Dade, Broward, and Volusia.

On November 10, the machine count was completed with Bush in the lead by only 327 votes; however, the count was not certified, and since the race was so tight, Palm Beach County officials voted to conduct a full *hand* count of the ballots, and the other three counties voted to do the same. Yet, Bush's legal team, led by former Secretary of State James Baker, went to court to stop the manual recount, along with other lawyers, who questioned the legality of certain absentee votes and other issues.

On November 13, Florida's Secretary of State, Katherine Harris, declared that she would not extend the November 14, 5 P.M. EST deadline for a recount of the votes. As Gore's team prepared another challenge, the Bush team's motion to stop the manual recount was defeated in court. This battle continued, in and out of court all the way to the United States Supreme Court, even after Harris certified the Florida vote on November 26, with Bush in the lead by 537 votes. After a United States Supreme Court ruling to halt all further counts in the state of Florida, Bush was the winner. To his 2,912,790 votes, Gore had received 2,912,253, Buchanan 17,412, and Nader came in third with 97,421 votes.

Then, the Democrats were really in an uproar. Had Nader dropped out of the race, they complained, his votes would have gone to Gore, giving Gore the Florida electoral votes he needed to win the Presidency. The *Los Angeles Times* reported, "According to a Florida exit poll, about half of Nader's supporters—mostly young white male liberals and moderates— would have voted for Gore had Nader not been on the ballot."[2] The Greens, however, disagreed with this statement. Their figures showed that about thirty percent of the people who voted for Nader were newly registered voters—who would not have participated in the election, except to vote for Nader—and twenty percent came from Bush. Forty percent were those who might have voted for Gore, if Nader had not run, which did not help their cause. The more than 38,000 votes would have put Gore over the top. Many pointed fingers at Nader. He had not gotten the five percent of the vote needed for the Green Party to attain matching funds from the government, and they saw no point to his candidacy, except to "spoil" the results. However, Nader adroitly defended the charges, and during the campaign had told reporters, "The polls indicate we're drawing from the Ross Perot voters, we're drawing from independent voters, and we're drawing from new voters who never voted before."[3] Nader cited his activities on college campuses for drawing in voters, coming into the political arena for the first time.

During an interview on National Public Radio, Nader later replied to Neal Conan's remark, "Unfortunately, part of your legacy looks like it's going to be putting George W. Bush in the White House."[4] Nader said,

You really believe that, in a winner-take-all system, a new political party should not mess up the likelihood of one or the other of the major candidates to win. And if you say that, I disagree with you. I don't think the political system can be regenerated from within anymore.... [The two parties] have had their chance every four years, and they seem to be getting more corrupt and more indifferent to the people's needs, and more subservient to corporate power. But if what you're saying is that we're stuck with a system that doesn't have proportional representation, it's a winner take all, so third parties don't clutter the field, then at least, I know where you're coming from.[5]

Nader still had an army of supporters. Author and staunch Naderite R. A. "Deck" Deckert wrote, "The Democrats forfeited the right to the automatic vote of progressives, liberals, and what Paul Wellstone[6] used to call 'the Democratic wing of the Democratic Party' a long time ago, and there is no sign that they intend to earn it back soon. They have sold their soul to the same fat cats as the Republicans have and totally ignored their base."[7]

THE CASE AGAINST MICROSOFT

A constant wrangling over whether or not Nader cost the Democrats the election would continue into the future; however, a cause that Nader had begun to fight before the election heated up after the election was over—the antitrust case against Microsoft.

In June 1990, the Federal Trade Commission (FTC) launched a probe into possible collusion between IBM and Microsoft. At that time, all new IBM PCs had the MS-DOS-based Windows operating system[8] installed and were sold to consumers, who were given no choice as to which type of operating system they wished to have on their new computers. Windows had become popular very fast, as rather than the completely keyboard-based operation with other operating systems, users were able to "point and click" with a mouse, rather than type in often lengthy command strings, as was necessary with older operating systems. Yet, consumers were not afforded a choice when buying an IBM computer. Other operating systems, such as Red Hat's Linux and Open Group's Unix were also available, but Microsoft Windows was dominating the field. Antitrust charges, filed in July 1994, alleged that Microsoft had used its dominance in the marketplace to further squelch the competition. The case was settled out of court when Microsoft signed a consent decree, which forbade the company to continue such practices as they had used with IBM. The agreement was approved in August 1995.

In October 1997, however, the Justice Department filed another complaint, charging that Microsoft had forced computer manufacturers to bundle Internet Explorer (IE), a World Wide Web browser, in with their hardware products, and had made it a mandatory companion to Windows 95 for computer manufacturers to obtain a resale license. In December, an injunction forced Microsoft to cease making IE a requirement for a Windows license and in January 1998, the company signed another agreement, giving computer makers freedom to install Windows 95 without installing IE. Yet, when Windows 98 was released, an appeals court ruled that Microsoft could integrate whatever it pleased into its own software, as long as it would benefit consumers and as long as it could not be imitated.

This prompted the U.S. Justice Department to file another antitrust lawsuit against Microsoft, citing Microsoft's power to thwart their competition, which included the Internet browser company Netscape. Up until that time, Netscape had a tidy browser share lead over any competition, including Microsoft. With Microsoft's innovations in Windows 98, that lead eroded until Internet Explorer superseded Netscape's popularity in September of 1998.

After an eight-month trial, Judge Thomas Penfield Jackson issued his finding that Microsoft held a monopoly and had used it to harm consumers and other companies. Talks to settle the case failed and Judge Jackson was petitioned to divide the company into two separate entities as retribution for its offense, which was so ordered on June 7, 2000. Yet, that was not to be Microsoft's final fate. When Jackson's decision was appealed on June 28, 2001, the breakup order was overturned. The case was finally settled on November 1, 2002, with the corporation ordered to provide competitors with detailed technical data to allow them to make competing products so that their software and/or equipment would run smoothly within the Windows environment. Microsoft was also ordered to offer a standard licensing agreement to all computer manufacturers and to remove desktop icons linking to add-on Windows features, such as Windows Media Player. This agreement still did not meet with the approval of Microsoft's competitors, however, and the legal battles still continue among the rival companies.

NADER'S ROLE

Nader firmly voiced his opposition to the Microsoft issue and the company's chairperson, Bill Gates. When asked why he was against Bill Gates, Nader said,

One, he's a monopolist, as the federal judge determined. His company is a monopolist. Two, he produces very mediocre software, as anybody who's tried to use it and avoid having it crash knows. But a monopoly of the operating system has allowed Microsoft to glue on application systems that it controls and that have suffered stagnation. I mean, when you keep the innovators off the railroad track, so to speak, stagnation inevitably follows in spreadsheets and presentation graphics and so forth.[9]

In 1998, Nader had come up with an idea to stop Microsoft outside the courtroom. He proposed that the government stop buying and using Microsoft software. In an article in *Computerworld*, Nader and James Love, the director of another Nader organization—the Consumer Project on Technology—wrote: "If the government can't curtail Microsoft's anticompetitive conduct in the browser market, the company gets the green light to become even bolder elsewhere."[10]

In 2002, Nader and Love wrote a letter to the Director of the Office of Management and Budget (OMB), stating precise ways in which to curtail Microsoft's monopoly in the software industry. They suggested that the OMB should force Microsoft to fully disclose file formats in the company's software, Microsoft Office, and in multimedia programs (Windows Media Player), allowing the programs to be read by other platforms, such as Apple, Linux, Oracle, and to look into purchasing other office suites, such as Corel's WordPerfect Office. They also recommended a cost analysis to determine the benefits of buying Microsoft's software code outright, rather than leasing it, and to consider the savings to taxpayers of not buying software full of bugs intentionally created by the corporation in order to force costly upgrading just to solve problems in the older code.

Many disagreed that the plan would work. In *Tech Update*, Dan Farber wrote, "But while your goals are worthy, the means are way off target."[11] Farber opined that Microsoft would move to another country, where there would be tax breaks and where the company could continue to sell computers and export them to the United States. "Remember," Farber wrote, "software is very lightweight and transportable. Microsoft could be up and running in a matter of days."[12] If people are so sick and tired of Microsoft, he suggests they should start protesting with their money by spending it on other office suites, operating systems, etc., as there are many other choices, but Microsoft continues because buyers want it. Nader continues to argue his case.

Nader doesn't see things changing for big business during the Bush administration either. When asked if he thought corporations were running the Bush administration, he replied,

> They don't have to control him, he is of them. It's a government that comes out of the corporate world. Forty-one top officials in the Bush administration hail from the oil and gas industry alone, so it's like the corporate executives moving in. One reporter said, 'Before Bush, corporations controlled the government. With Bush, they've moved in to run it.' So, it's not like he's some president who's reluctantly under the influence, he's one of them...He is overwhelmingly a corporatist president, more dedicated to a government of the General Motors by the Exxon's for the DuPonts, than he is of, by and for the people or the workers or the consumers. And he continues in his policies to verify and validate that impression and in the way he's raising money all over the country in such torrents of business money that he doesn't even have to consider taking public money after the primaries, as he's entitled to do, because it's not enough for him. He can raise much more [through big business].[13]

And in Nader's view, the debacle over Enron is a prime example.

A HOUSE OF TOOTHPICKS

In July 1985, Houston Natural Gas merged with InterNorth of Omaha, thereby integrating 40,000 miles of pipeline to create the first national natural gas system in the United States. In 1986, it was decided that the new company's name would be Enron and economist and former Houston Natural Gas CEO Kenneth Lay would be its chairman and chief executive officer. When deregulation of the energy business came along with the Reagan administration in the 1980s, Lay envisioned not only a natural gas company, but one that would engender an energy trading revolution. Rather than just a supplier, the company would act as a broker, selling and buying tomorrow's gas at a fixed price, thus guaranteeing stable prices for consumers, while making a tidy profit.

In 1987, however, the company learned that New York oil traders had overextended Enron's accounts by nearly $1 billion. Although it was a nasty blow, the company continued to do so well that it was able to work the loss down to $142 million the same year. To counteract such losses again, Enron diversified and became involved in brokering many different commodities, including advertising space, steel, and coal. The company was becoming so successful that it expanded to the United Kingdom and India, and even acquired new pipeline in South America.

Enron had strong political connections to George H. W. and George W. Bush, via Lay's personal relationship with the two men. And as Enron expanded, there was little government scrutiny of how its business was being carried out. As the dot.com business grew in the late 1990s, Enron planned to move into broadband Internet networks and to trade bandwidth capacity, along with its other commodities. In 1999, it opened Enron Online, an Internet commodity-trading site, and as Enron's business grew, investors began to appreciate its bold moves into the new economy, accompanied by its strong roots in traditional business, and the company's share price soared. Enron Energy Services showed its first profit in the fourth quarter of 1999.

Yet, the world of Internet trading was less than stable and Enron became secretive about its online trading. Around this time, it is believed that the company began procedures not in accordance with generally accepted accounting principles in order to keep its share price high. Enron increased investments against its own assets and stock in order to maintain the guise of a healthy company. In 2000, it invested in Enron Field in Houston, home of the Huston Astros, and with investors IBM and America Online, launched a new company—The New Power Company—to provide electric services. Based on such prodigious capitalization, the Energy Financial Group ranked Enron as the sixth-largest energy company in the world and the 2000 annual report showed earnings of $100 billion, a 40 percent increase in income in only three years.

But all was not as it seemed on the surface. Enron continued to make investments and then shift the debt off their books to "independent" partnerships, code-named Raptors, in return for future income that would buffer future losses. To entice investors, Enron quietly pledged blocks of its own stock to the Raptors to further guarantee against losses, which was a dangerous action. If the price of Enron's stock dropped below $20 a share, it would not be able to cover its obligations, and the Raptors would fail. In addition, for every dollar below $20 that Enron's stock price fell, the company would have to absorb $124 million in losses. Yet at the outset of the plan, the leaders at Enron saw only money. A top executive said, "We're the world's coolest company."[14]

Enron also continued to make hefty political contributions, a large part of which came from Lay himself. Both the company and Lay contributed $100,000 to then President-elect George W. Bush's inaugural committee fund in January 2001, and Lay was invited to be part of Bush's transition team for entering the White House.

However, Lay was concerned over the incoming administration's proposed energy policy review, which was to be headed by Vice President Dick Cheney. As a prelude to this review, Lay and Enron directors met three times with Cheney between the January inauguration and April 2001, and though Cheney's review was ultimately favorable to the energy industry, that same year things began to unravel.

In February, Jeff Skilling, who had come to Enron in 1990, was named chief executive officer, while Ken Lay remained as chairperson. Skilling had created the "gas bank," whereby Enron bought natural gas in large quantities from producers at a low price and resold it for a profit to other gas companies, which Enron held to long-term contracts. This actually stabilized the gas market in the United States, increased gas production, and gave Enron enormous profits in the early years of its inception.

Yet, Skilling was also behind the Raptor arrangement, which was initiated by Andrew Fastow, Enron's chief financial officer. Fastow encouraged Enron to open a partnership in the Cayman Islands,[15] which could protect the company's investment in Rhythms NetConnections. The dot.com had netted Enron $300 million in revenue, and the plan was to allow the proposed partnership to hedge the Rhythms investment and to lock in the gain for Enron by supporting any losses with Enron stock. Ordinarily, Wall Street firms provide this insurance service for a fee, but as a dot.com, Rhythms was a risky investment and no company would insure it. Enron perceived the need to maintain the thirty percent in profit standings that Rhythms provided, so in essence, Enron insured itself. If Rhythms stock fell, Enron would bolster the loss with its own shares.

Outside financial advisors, including Enron's accounting firm, Arthur Andersen LLP, were against the plan, as the risk was huge. In the event of both stocks tumbling, the arrangement could lead to disaster. To make matters worse, Fastow was personally involved in the scheme. Though a conflict of interest in the arrangement was evident, he not only invested in the offshore partnership, but he named it LJM, after his wife and two children.

Though these red flags were flying high, Skilling and Fastow were able to push this shaky arrangement through Enron's board of directors, and the plan was put into motion. Skilling told the University of Virginia business school in 2000, "We like risk because you make money by taking risk. The key is to take on risk that you manage better than your competitors."[16]

In March, a deal with Blockbuster to provide movies over the Internet fell through and in April, Enron disclosed a $570 million debt, caused by the bankruptcy of California's Pacific Gas and Electric. That was bad enough, but still things got worse.

In May, Clifford Baxter, an Enron executive, left the company. It was rumored that he had clashed with Skilling over the questionable partnership transactions. Later, Baxter would take his own life, perhaps over the mess brewing in Enron. Dozens of layoffs came to Enron employees. Then, Skilling told Lay that he wanted to resign to spend more time with his family, that the pressure of running Enron had gotten to him, and he had trouble sleeping. His resignation was completed on August 14 and Lay resumed the position of CEO.

These events, accompanied by news of the New Power Company's disappointing earnings (which dropped the company's stock price by thirty percent), worried investors, who began to suspect that Enron's meteoric rise was built on a foundation of cards. They sold millions of shares of Enron stock, taking the price of stock down four dollars in one week, and as the price continued to plummet, Lay continued to reassure investors that there was nothing wrong, though he had been warned by an executive, who knew of Baxter's concerns, that the company was about to implode.

In September 2001, the Enron–Arthur Andersen partnership was unraveling over the "cross-collateralization" of Enron's partnership dealings, by the fact that the company was making loans that were not disclosed as such, but recorded as energy transactions, and because Andersen viewed that the company had no long-range plans. It seemed as though Enron's leaders were simply operating from quarter to quarter, looking for earnings to keep their stock well priced. "In 2000 alone," the *Washington Post* reported, "$296 million, or thirty percent of the profit that Enron recorded in its annual report to shareholders, came from one-time tax-saving strategies rather than the company's energy supply and trading businesses."[17] Andersen worried that a government investigation of Enron was nearing, and since they had recently been fined for allowing another large company (Waste Management, Inc.) to issue illusory financial statements, they worried about their involvement in the Enron fiasco. An executive in Andersen's Houston office told colleagues to destroy any unneeded documents, and the shredding began, of both paper and electronic communications.

When Enron released its third-quarter earnings in October, there were $1.01 billion in charges, which included $35 million in investment "Raptor" partnerships, headed by Andrew Fastow. He was quickly replaced as chief financial officer, and the unraveling began when the Securities and Exchange Commission started an investigation of Enron's financial underpinnings.

On December 2, Enron filed for bankruptcy protection. Its share price had fallen from a high of more than $90 to being worth less than $1, and in January 2002, a criminal investigation was begun by the U.S. Justice Department. Attorney General John Ashcroft, who had received campaign contributions from Enron in 2000, exempted himself from the process. The White House also admitted that Lay had contacted members of the Bush administration for aid. An internal investigation pinned the blame for the company's demise on its executives, who took the Fifth Amendment rather than testify before Congress. Skilling testified, but claimed no knowledge of the complex Raptor arrangements; however, Sherron Watkins, who first brought the fiasco to the attention of Lay and senior Enron management, after Skilling's departure, testified that Skilling and Fastow had deceived Lay, who never understood the complexity of and the potential dangers of the financial arrangements made by his staff.

In the end, Arthur Andersen was found guilty of obstruction of justice, and its business fell apart. The trust required of an accounting firm had eroded sufficiently to cause most of Andersen's clients to terminate their relationship with the firm, causing the firm to file bankruptcy and cease operating soon thereafter. Enron's CFO Fastow pleaded guilty to six felony conspiracy and fraud charges and received a 10-year sentence without possibility of parole. Skilling was indicted by the SEC on February 19, 2004, and pleaded not guilty to an array of thirty-five charges including fraud, securities fraud, and of making false statements to auditors. Only Kenneth Lay remains unaffected, but speculation is that he will also be indicted.

Of the debacle, Nader said, "I hate to say, 'I told you so,' but...I told you so."[18] Yet, he sees this as an opportunity for the public to become more astutely aware of the impacts of corporate crime, which he has always felt should carry prison sentences for those involved. "Enron is our engine for reform," he said. "Enron is the supermarket of corporate crime for our time.... The politicians are scrambling to explain why they took those checks from Ken Lay."[19] Yet, he does not feel that there are adequate resources for the Justice Department to handle cases such as Enron and a similar situation involving WorldCom, another mega-corporation that crumbled due to bad business, adequately:

> They're prosecuting some of these high-profile cases, but the problem is that if the Justice Department and the White House were really serious about cracking down on corporate crime, fraud, and abuse, they would very significantly expand the

number of FBI agents and Justice Department lawyers and investigators, working exclusively on corporate crime and they've not done that. Their corporate crime crew in the Justice Department is miniscule compared to the magnitude of the corporate crime wave that has swept the country in the last three years and drained or looted trillions of dollars from millions of workers, small investors, and their pension plans and also caused considerable unemployment, like the lay-offs following the Enron collapse.

So that is really the test. It isn't the rhetoric coming out of the President. It isn't the few high-profile indictments. It's how many federal cops do they have on the corporate crime beat? And that is extremely small. The potential doubling of the SEC budget does not affect that because the SEC does not bring criminal cases, it transmits them over to the Justice Department, and that's where the cul-de-sac is. So, you can have a bigger SEC. But in terms of criminal prosecution, it doesn't mean anything, other than perhaps more cases referred to the Justice Department, which they cannot handle.

The case on WorldCom will absorb a large number of the available Justice Department lawyers and all these companies have a significantly larger number of lawyers representing them through these corporate law firms. The tiny crew in the Justice Department is up against thousands and thousands of corporate lawyers. WorldCom probably has a thousand lawyers representing them in a variety of ways. So, in the entire Anti-Trust division of the Justice department, they have about 450 lawyers. That's not the [division of] corporate crime, but that's one of the biggest collections of lawyers in the Justice Department.[20]

Corporate crime is not the only item on Nader's agenda in the year 2004. Several of the changes that have come because of the tragedy of September 11, 2001 to him are appalling. He worries about the loss of freedom the American people have experienced at the hands of the new security measures taken since that time and condemns the Patriot Act as unconstitutional:

The Patriot Act is much too extreme in curtailing and showing civil liberties in this country, in the name of fighting terrorism, and it has many provisions, and very vague standards which I think would be declared unconstitutional or certainly should. For example, arresting people without charges and putting them in jail without lawyers, taking material witnesses and jailing them without releasing their names or allowing them to have council. All of these are completely contradictory to America's jurisprudential tradition of civil liberties, due process, and probable cause. And this is being done not just [to] immigrants or [to] people who are permanent residents, but [to] American citizens, as well. Also, it's chilling free speech, it's chilling the Democrat opposition and it's destroying a significant dimension of freedoms that Bush is alleging he is protecting and that's the dilemma. Considerations of security are vastly expanded at the expense of freedom and civil liberties and free speech without really producing much of a successful catch rate.

It's increasingly clear that all these violations of civil liberties has not really caught any real terrorists trying to blow up this and that. They've caught people who've been accused of sending money to charities and they've been forced to cop pleas. Some of them have been incarcerated and had to be released, with egg on the faces of the prosecutors, because they didn't have a shred of evidence. Others were accused of going to this meeting and that. This is a typical type of sloppy enforcement, called dragnet enforcement, which substitutes either inability or incompetence in finding the real thing and maybe the real thing wasn't there. Maybe the threat was wildly exaggerated after 9/11. Certainly, as certain Security experts have told me that if Bush and Ashcroft are right, and there are Al Quaida cells all over the United States that are funded, hateful, suicidal and are being hunted by thousands of federal agents, why haven't they struck back, since by all accounts we have a very complex industrial economy that is very vulnerable at many, many points?

So, while one doesn't want to underestimate threats, the exaggeration of threats for political advantage to the leaders of the Bush administration is hard for them to resist. They have so many pluses—they keep up in the polls, they chill or silence the Democrats, they make the munitions companies and the oil companies very happy, the whole industry is around those governmental contracts. They focus attention overseas and distract attention from serious domestic necessities in this country that Bush has never felt comfortable or interested in confronting or responding to.[21]

In mid-August 2003, Nader's negative fervor regarding the Bush administration suggested another try for president in 2004, but he would not commit. "I really haven't decided yet," he said. "I'm checking on various things, seeing what opportunities there are."[22] Shortly thereafter, a new Web site opened: http://www.votenader.org, where Nader asked for people's opinions on whether or not he should run. He wanted feedback, and the response was positive. All the pieces fell into place. Nader announced his candidacy for the presidential election on February 23, 2004, though this time, he would not be running as a Green, but as an independent. "After careful thought and my desire to retire our supremely elected president," Nader said on NBC, in a reference to the Supreme Court decision that settled the 2000 presidential race, "I've decided to run as an independent candidate for president."[23]

Of course, duopoly is not the be-all and end-all of American government. Nader provides a new voice for change, perhaps change for the better. An administration with no ties to big business might allow for a brave new society to develop—where men and women, rather than faceless, greedy companies with no consideration for the human spirit, make the rules. Nader in 2004. A possibility or just a dream?

Regardless of the outcome of this election, Nader will continue to move forward. He will continue to be a true *citizen* of the world until the day he dies, working for the common good. As Nathra Nader often said, "If you don't use your rights, you'll lose your rights."[24] How many of us are already in danger?

NOTES

1. Quoted in Eun-Kyung Kimand, Jonathan D. Salant, "Nader Lacks Needed 5%," *Associated Press*, 8 November 2000, p. A-19.

2. Scott Martelle, "Unrepentant Ralph Nader Shuns the Mantle of Spoiler," *Los Angeles Times*, 9 November 2000, p. A-14.

3. Ralph Nader, News Conference, *FDCH Political Transcripts*, 25 October 2000.

4. Neal Conan, "Interview: Ralph Nader Discusses His Campaign and His Future, as Well as the Future of the Green Party," *Talk of the Nation* (National Public Radio), 11 November 2000. http://web4.epnet.com/

5. Conan, "Interview: Ralph Nader Discusses His Campaign."

6. Democratic United States Senator from Minnesota, who was killed in an airplane crash in 2002.

7. Deck Deckert, "It's All Nader's Fault and Other Fairy Tales," *Swans Commentary*, 1 September 2003, http://www.swams.com/library/art9/rdeck044.html.

8. Software that controls the hardware inside the computer, such as sound card, hard drive, CD-ROM, and so forth.

9. Nader, News Conference, 25 October 2000.

10. Ralph Nader and James Love, "Opinion: Ralph Nader Tells Feds to Stop Microsoft," *Computerworld*, 11 November 1998, http://www.cnn.com/TECH/computing/9811/11/nader.idg/

11. Dan Farber, "What's Wrong with Nader's Microsoft Plan," *Tech Update*, 5 June 2002, http://techupdate.zdnet.com/techupdate/stories/main/0,14179,2869443,00.html.

12. Farber, "What's Wrong with Nader's Microsoft Plan."

13. Ralph Nader, interview with the author, 15 August 2003.

14. Quoted in Peter Behr and April Witt, "Visionary's Dream Led to Risky Business," *Washington Post*, 28 July 2002, p. A01.

15. Companies establish operations in offshore markets, primarily for favorable taxation levels, but also for information and asset protection, mainly from the government.

16. Behr and Witt, "Visionary's Dream Led to Risky Business," p. A01.

17. Peter Bahr and April Witt, "Concerns Grow Amid Conflicts," *Washington Post*, 30 July 2002, p. A01.

18. Quoted in John Nichols, "Enron? Nader Is Glad You Asked," *The Nation*, 25 February 2002, http://www.thenation.com/doc.mhtml?I=20020225&s=nichols.

19. Quoted in Nichols, "Enron? Nader Is Glad You Asked."

20. Nader, interview with the author, 15 August 2003.

21. Nader, interview with the author, 15 August 2003.

22. Nader, interview with the author, 15 August 2003.

23. Quoted in "Nader announces Presidential Run," *CNN.com*, 23 February 2004, http://www.cnn.com/2004/ALLPOLITICS/02,22,elec04.prez.nader.

24. Rose B. Nader and Nathra Nader. *It Happened in the Kitchen. Recipes for Food and Thought* (Washington, D.C.: Center for Study of Responsive Law, 1991), p. 155.

SELECTED BIBLIOGRAPHY

PRIMARY WORKS

Green, Mark J., with Beverly C. Moore, Jr. and Bruce Wasserstein. *The Closed Enterprise System, Ralph Nader's Study Group Report on Antitrust Enforcement*. New York: Grossman, 1972.

Green, Mark, ed. *Verdicts on Lawyers*. New York: Crowell, 1976.

Greider, William, Margaret Atwood, David Philips, and Pat Choate. *The Case Against "Free Trade": GATT, NAFTA, and the Globalization of Corporate Power*. Ralph Nader, ed. Berkeley, CA: North Atlantic Books, 1993.

Isaac, Katherine. *Ralph Nader Presents Civics for Democracy, a Journey for Teachers and Students*. Washington, D.C.: Essential Information, 1992.

Nader, Ralph. *Crashing the Party: Taking on the Corporate Government in an Age of Surrender*. New York: St. Martin's Press, 2002.

———. *Cutting Corporate Welfare*. New York: Seven Stories, 2000.

———. *Unsafe at Any Speed, the Designed-In Dangers of the American Automobile*. New York: Grossman, 1965.

Nader, Ralph, and John Abbotts. *The Menace of Atomic Energy*. Rev. ed. New York: Norton, 1979.

Nader, Ralph, Ronald Brownstein, and John Richard, eds. *Who's Poisoning America: Corporate Polluters and Their Victims in the Chemical Age*. San Francisco: Sierra Club Books, 1981.

Nader, Ralph, and Clarence Ditlow, with Laura Polacheck and Tamar Rhode. *The Lemon Book, Auto Rights*. 3rd ed. Mount Kisco, NY: Moyer Bell, 1990.

Nader, Ralph, and Mark J. Green, ed. *The Monopoly Makers, Ralph Nader's Study Group Report on Regulation and Competition*. New York: Grossman, 1973.

Nader, Ralph, and Donald Ross, with Brent English and Joseph Highland. *Action for a Change, A Student's Manual for Public Interest Organizing.* New York: Grossman, 1971.

Nader, Ralph, and Wesley J. Smith. *No Contest, Corporate Lawyers and the Perversion of Justice in America.* New York: Random House, 1996.

Nader, Ralph, and William Taylor. *The Big Boys: Power and Position in American Business.* New York: Random House, 1986.

Nader, Ralph, Lori Wallach, and Patrick Woodall. *Whose Trade Organization? A Comprehensive Guide to the World Trade Organization.* 2nd ed. New York: New Press, 2004.

Page, Joseph A., and Mary-Win O'Brien. *Bitter Wages, Ralph Nader's Study Group Report on Disease and Injury on the Job.* New York: Grossman, 1973.

SECONDARY WORKS

Documents

Public Law 59–384. Federal Food and Drugs Act of 1906. The U.S. Food and Drug Administration. http://www.fda.gov/opacom/laws/wileyact.htm.

Books

Asch, Peter. *Consumer Safety Regulation: Putting a Price on Life and Limb.* New York: Oxford University Press, 1988.

Baer, M. Delal, and Sidney Weintraub, eds. *NAFTA Debate: Grappling with Unconventional Trade Issues.* Boulder, CO: Lynne Rienner, 1994.

Berry, Jeffrey M. *The New Liberalism: The Rising Power of Citizen Groups.* Washington, D.C.: Brookings Institution, 1999.

Bourne, Peter G. *Jimmy Carter, a Comprehensive Biography from Plains to Postpresidency.* New York: Lisa Drew/Scribner, 1997.

Carter, Luther J. *Nuclear Imperatives and Public Trust: Dealing with Radioactive Waste.* Washington, D.C.: Resources for the Future, 1987.

Churchill, Ward, and Jim Vander. *The CONINTELPRO Papers.* Cambridge, MA: South End Press, 1990.

Collins, Susan M., ed. *Imports, Exports, and the American Worker.* Washington, D.C.: Brookings Institution Press, 1998.

Doyle, Jack. *Taken for a Ride: Detroit's Big Three and the Politics of Pollution.* New York: Four Walls Eight Windows, 2000.

Gorey, Hays. *Nader and the Power of Everyman.* New York: Grosset & Dunlap, 1975.

Harris, Fred R. *The New Populism.* New York: Saturday Review Press, 1973.

Hoeveler, J. David. "Populism, Politics, and Public Policy: 1970s Conservatism." *Loss of Confidence: Politics and Policy in the 1970s*, ed. David Brian Robertson, 10:75–98. University Park: Pennsylvania State University Press, 1998.

Keith, Michael C., and Robert L. Hilliard. *Low-Power Television in America*. Armonk, NY: M. E. Sharpe, 1999.

Morris, Kenneth E. *Jimmy Carter, American Moralist*. Athens: University of Georgia Press, 1996.

Samli, A. Coskun. *Social Responsibility in Marketing: a Proactive and Profitable Marketing Management Strategy*. Westport, CT: Quorum Books, 1992.

Shales, Tom, and James Andrew Miller. *Live from New York*. Boston: Little, Brown, 2002.

Skurski, Roger, ed. *New Directions in Economic Justice*. Notre Dame, IN: University of Notre Dame Press, 1983.

White, G. Edward. *Tort Law in America: An Intellectual History*. New York: Oxford University Press, 1980.

PERIODICALS

Anonymous. "Globalization in Historical Perspective." *World Economic Outlook*, May 1997, 112–38.

Anonymous. "Ralph Nader: A Conversation." *American Prospect*, 19 June 2000, 15.

Barnes, Fred. "No Saint." *New Republic*, 16 December 1985, 50.

Bordo, Michael D. "Is There a Good Case for a New Bretton Woods International Monetary System?" *American Economic Review* 85, no. 2, May 1995: 317–22.

Briar-Lawson, Katharine. "Capacity Building for Integrated Family-Centered Practice." *Social Work* 43, no. 6, November 1998: 539.

Brimelow, Peter, and Leslie Spencer. "Ralph Nader, Inc." *Forbes*, 17 September 1990, 117–25.

Bruner, M. Lane. "Global Constitutionalism and the Arguments over Free Trade." *Communication Studies* 53, no. 1, Spring 2002: 25–39.

Conniff, Ruth. "Joan Claybrook." *Progressive*, March 1999, 33.

Dunham, Wayne R. "Are Automobile Safety Regulations Worth the Price: Evidence from Used Car Markets." *Economic Inquiry* 35, vol 35, no. 3, July 1997: 579–89.

England, R. S. "Congress, Nader, and the Ambulance Chasers." *American Spectator*, September 1990, 18–24.

Holsendorf, Ernest. "Nader Calls on Ex-Colleague to Resign Safety Post." *New York Times*, 1 December 1977, 18.

Nader, Ralph. "After Enron." *Progressive*, March 2002, 18.
———. "Beware the History Books." *Progressive*, April 1995, 26–27.
———. "Organizing People: The One Sure Way to Defeat Enronism." *American Prospect* 25, March 2002, 18–19.
———. "Overcoming the Oligarchy." *Progressive*, January 1999, 58.
———. "The Democrats Bow to the Megabanks." *Progressive*, January 2000, 24.
Nader, Ralph, and James Love. "Looting the Medicine Chest: How Bristol-Myers Squibb Made off with the Public's Cancer Research." *Progressive*, February 1993, 26+.
Nader, Ralph, and Wesley J. Smith. "Uncle Sam's Corporate Lawyers." *Washington Monthly*, October 1996, 26–27.
Rowe, Jonathan. "Ralph Nader Reconsidered." *Washington Monthly*, February 1989, 29–33.
Rowe, Jonathan, and Steven Waldman. "Beyond Money: Replacing the Gold Standard with the Golden Rule." *Washington Monthly*, May 1990, 32–40.
Seis, Mark. "Confronting the Contradiction: Global Capitalism and Environmental Health." *International Journal of Comparative Sociology*, February–May 2001, 123.
Sneider, Daniel. "Clash of Titans in California Over Limiting Lawsuits." *Christian Science Monitor*, 15 March 1996, 1.
Spencer, L. "The Tort Tax." *Forbes*, 17 February 1992, 40–42.
Tarry, Scott E. "Issue Definition, Conflict Expansion, and Tort Reform: Lessons from the American General Aviation Industry." *Policy Studies Journal* 29, no. 4: 57–73.

Internet Sources

Appalachian Power.com. http://www.appalachaianpower.com/.
Avalon Project at Yale Law. http://www.yale.edu/lawweb/avalon.
Bell's Palsy InfoSite &Forums. http://www.bellspalsy.ws.
Bureau of Labor Statistics. http://data.bls.gov.
Business Rountable. http://www.businessroundtable.org.
Connecticut Historical Society. http://www.chs.org.
Dunn, James A., Jr. *Driving Forces: The Automobile, Its Enemies, and the Politics of Mobility.* Brookings Institution Press, 1998. http://brookings.nap.edu/books/.
Energy Information Administration. http://www.eia.doe.gov.
Federal Communications Commission. http://www.fcc.gov.
Federal Election Commission. http://www.fec.gov/.

Fehner, Terrence R., and Jack M. Hall. "Department of Energy 1977–1994, Summary History." *US Department of State*. http://www.4uth.gov.ua/usa/english/politics/cabinet/doehist.htm.

Funesti, Bob. "Reflections of the 1966 Congressional Hearings to Establish a Department of Transportation." *National Transportation and Safety Administration*. 30 June 1997. http://www.nhtsa.dot.gov/nhtsa/announce/nhtsanow/v3.9/.

Gilbert School. http://www.gilbertschool.org/academics.html.

Janssen, Wallace F. "The Story of the Laws Behind the Labels." *Food and Drug Administration, FDA Consumer*. June 1981. http://vm.cfsan.fda.gov/~lrd/history1.html.

Jimmy Carter Library and Museum. http://www.jimmycarterlibrary.org/

Nader, Ralph. "Ralph Nader on Tort Reform." *Legal Times*. 1995. http://www.lectlaw.com.

National Archives. http://www.archives.gov.

Princeton Project 55. http://www.nfid.org/fctsheets/princeton55.html.

Smith, Wesley R. "The NAFTA Debate, Part 1: A Primer on Labor, Environmental, and Legal Issues." *Backgrounder*. 9 April 1993. http://www.heritage.org/Research/TradeandForeignAid/BG036.cfm.

The *President Reagan Information Page*. http://www.presidentreagan.info/

Timedollars.org. http://www.timedollar.org.

U.S. Census. http://www.census.gov.

Wessell, Nils Y. "Remembering Daniel Patrick Moynihan." *Tufts Journal*. May 2003. http://tuftsjournal.tufts.edu/archive/2003/may/oped/index.shtml.

World Trade Organization. http://www.wto.org.

INDEX

About the Author

PATRICIA CRONIN MARCELLO is a freelance writer who lives in Florida with her husband and daughter. She has written eight books, including biographies of Gloria Steinem (Greenwood, 2004), the Dalai Lama (Greenwood, 2003), and Princess Diana. She has also written for national and regional publications and was an instructor for the Institute of Children's Literature for more than five years.